BRADFORDSVILLIANS

History
Shenanigans
Legends & Ghost Stories

By

Jeanette Wooley Wilson, primary writer

First edition 2018

Bradfordsvillians: History, Shenanigans, Legends & Ghost Stories
By Bradfordsville Historical Society

Copyright ©2018 by Bradfordsville Historical Society
Printed On-Demand

All rights reserved. No part of this publication may be reproduced, stored in a retrieval system, or transmitted in any form or by any means—electronic, mechanical, photocopy, recording, or any other—except for brief quotations in printed reviews, without the prior permission of the copyright holder.

Softcover ISBN 978-1-64338-054-4

24 Hours Books, Inc.
14 S. Queen Street, Mt. Sterling, Kentucky 40353, USA
www.24hourbooks.co
Email orders@24hourbooks.co
Orders 1-800-765-2464
Information 859-520-3757
Text 606-359-2064
Printed and bound in the United States of America

PREFACE

Bradfordsvillians have always had the ability to laugh at themselve and with others. We thought it would be fitting to include in this book some of the earlier shenanigans carried on in and about the Bradfordsville community. For years we have laughed among ourselves and now we think it is time we share with others. There's nothing like laughs to clear the cobwebs from our minds and give our spirits a lift. Our stories aren't meant to offend anyone. As in all good stories there must be some embellishments in the telling. We are certain the reader will find some of that in these stories.

Most of the first section about our history was written by David Edelen and was derived from The Bradfordsville Historical Society's records on file at the Bradfordsville Learning Center. The writing style of the section Shenanigans can be attributed mostly to Jeanette Wooley Wilson. The shenanigans came from memories shared by several members and past members of the Bradfordsville community.

This book is written not only for entertainment but to convey the history of Bradfordsville to those who desire to know more about how this town came into being and about the citizens who played major roles in its development.

We hope you find this small book worth your reading, and we also hope you find yourself chuckling about adventures, some of which have never before been told.

The Bradfordsville Historical Society

Some current citizens of Bradfordsville

TABLE OF CONTENTS

History	9
Pre-Settlement	10
Introduction	13
Section I: Beginning of the Town	15
Section II: Civil War	18
Section III: Reconstruction	21
Section IV: Bradfordsville School Strike	24
Shenanigans	31
Clyde Wilson's Flagrant Son	32
The Morgesons	38
Buster Was a Jokester	40
Perry and the Hotdogs	40
The Mysterious Leaf	42
A Bird, A Snake, No, It's a Child	43
Ida Belle	44
My Baby Groundhogs	45
Right Out of the Sky	47
Long Names	49
Do You Remember Me?	50
Peeing Over the Farm Gate	52
Bucket of Fire	52
Buick Climbs the Steps	53
Where's My Girdle	54

TABLE OF CONTENTS, CONT'D

Cruising Down the River	55
Not in My Window	57
Skinny Dipping	58
Daring Willard Rakes	59
Pets	61
Nicknames	61
Biggest Foot in Town	62
To Pick up a Body	62
A Little Early	63
Tar Baby	64
Make a House Scream	64
Constable Ray Allstot	65
Air Horns	66
Halloween Pranks	67
Horse Sense	68
Reason to Court Again	68
Eight-Year-Old Flies	69
What's in my Bed?	70
Forgetter and Wading Boots	71
Sweet Susan Mann	72
A Car! Where?	73
Night of the World's Demise	74
Back at You and Run!	75
Tossing Compliments	76

TABLE OF CONTENTS, CONT'D

Put It on My Tombstone	76
Don't Keep Goldia Waiting	76
Pretty Vase for the New Table	77
Boy Scouts	78
The Scooter	79
The Water Tank	81
Swinging on the Grapevine	82
Shoe Cans	83
Sparkplug	83
Legends & Ghost Stories	**85**
My Encounter with an Angel	86
Light in the Narrows	88
Light in the Chimney	89
Grave Digger	89
Mamie Thurman	90
Phantom Horses	92
The "Japs" Have Landed	93
Cold as Clay	94
Mama's Visions	96
Gold on Travis Creek	98
The Spirit of Bradfordsville	100
Points of Interest	101

HISTORY

A people without the knowledge of their past history, origin and culture is like a tree without roots.

Marcus Garvey

PRE-SETTLEMENT

Native Americans had favorite hunting grounds near what was to become Bradfordsville. Two of their favorite trails were through Medlock Creek and Old Lick Gap. Several tribes used these trails. The Cherokees, Creeks, Chickamaugas and Chickasaws came in from the South. Shawnees and other tribes north of the Ohio 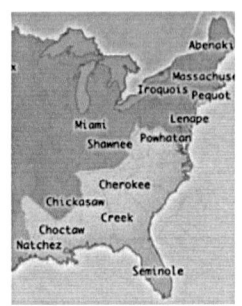 also used these trails. There have been found much evidence of Indian camps near Spurlington and on the summit of Muldaughs Hill. Even in the 30s and 40s, farmers plowing in the low lands near North, South and Rolling Fork Rivers found arrow point heads and spear heads. Flint implements were scattered everywhere.

No doubt a favorite camping ground or headquarters of the Native Americans during their hunting season was in this part of the state. Under the shelving rocks and cliffs of the South Rolling Fork, and North Fork as well, have been found fragments of pottery, some pieces nearly perfect, and graves with skeletons, pottery and shells, also teeth and fragments of different animals. In many places in the vicinity stone axes, pelts, pestles, discoidal stones and many of the smaller and more common implements have been found.

Passing through this territory on one or more occasions, after several settlements had been formed, the Indians perpetrated savage outrages upon our pioneer settlements. Bessie Taul Conkwright of the Louisville Times tells these stories that came from the oral history of the Coppage family.

William Coppage, son of Moses and Jane Coppage, was nearly killed by Indians in the early settlement years. Three miles above present Bradfordsville a fort had been established on the North Fork River. (This fort came to be known as the Kinnet Fort).

It was in this area that William Coppage, brother of James and Travis Sr., in company with Moses Mann was out prospecting to see if there were any Indians in the neighborhood. They were in a flat near present Casey and Marion county line when an Indian shot William through the shoulder. There were three Indians, two taking "the flank" with the other running directly after William. Running hard, William ran down to the mouth of Needmore Branch, then up the branch with the Indians in pursuit. They pressed him so hard that he threw his gun and shot-pouch in a sink hole and from there ran to the head of Casey Creek, thence to the head of Robinson Creek through Maple swamp, to the gap at the head of Sprewell's Branch, then up the branch with the Indians still pursuing to the South Fork, down that fork to Daniel Purdy's spring. He stopped just long enough to drink from the spring, leaving blood stains on the rocks. Then going down the Narrows above present Bradfordsville, he crossed over to the fort on the North Fork. Next morning after his arrival the people of the fort had assembled with their "tools" to go in search of Moses Mann, supposing he had been killed but, about this time Moses Mann appeared on the scene sound and safe!

William Coppage later moved to Missouri and settled there. He lived to be a very old man and drank whiskey and chewed tobacco all his life.

Moses Mann later moved into what is now Taylor County. He was the founder of Mannsville, Kentucky. He came to Kentucky in the latter part of 1700 and settled then in what is now Marion County, where he built a "palisade fort" and resided for several years. He was a Revolutionary War veteran. Alter settling in Kentucky, he and a man named Coppage were "Indian Scouts" and engaged in hunting and Indian fighting from the Rolling Fork to the Cumberland River.

While still living at the fort on the North Rolling Fork another terrible tragedy happened! Asa, Moses son, and Moses' hired man went night fishing with Nathaniel Carpenter on the Rolling Fork. They were attacked by Indians! Asa and the hired man were killed and Nathaniel, scalped, was left for dead, but he *recovered consciousness and crawled to Moses' stockade. He recovered but with less than satisfactory results; thereafter, he was irregularly bald and had to live with the loss of one ear.*

After the killing of his son, Asa, and his hired man, and the scalping of Nathaniel Carpenter, Moses "swore vengeance" and carried out his oath with considerable success. He was a skilled hunter and paid for several thousands of acres of land through his skill with the rifle.

He settled on Robinson Creek near the present village of Mannsville. He engaged in farming, stock raising, and salt manufacturing. He was 97 years old when he died and his wife, Fanny Bland, was 87 at her death.

During the same time of the Mann killing on the Rolling Fork the Indians butchered a family by the name Sloan above the junction of the North and South Fork Rivers. They burned the house and all that were in it. Not long after the massacre of the Sloan family, a family named Miller, living in perhaps the same neighborhood of the slaughter of the Sloan family where Bradfordsville now stands, was attacked by the Indians. Several were killed and others were carried off. About two years afterward those of the Miller family carried off were recaptured and returned to their friends.

Fort walls

INTRODUCTION

How do you describe being a "Bradfordsvillian"? It sounds so simple to us who live here, but it is very difficult to actually give a definition or give meaning to what a "Bradfordsvillian" really is.

The geographical limits of Bradfordsville are formed from the North Fork and South Fork Rivers coming together to form the Rolling Fork River, to the local mail route that claims three counties, Casey, Taylor and Marion, and including, too, along highways 49 going toward Lebanon and 1157 going toward Calvary.

Describing a "Bradfordsvillian" using such geographical means is too limited in its expression. The definition involves so much more to the mind, body, heart and soul. Once you become a Bradfordsvillian, it is very hard to let go; you seem to always identify yourself that way throughout your life.

History must first be considered when studying the Bradfordsvillian. Native Americans knew the area before Caucasians ever laid eyes on the territory. They knew of the beauty of the valley. They hunted in the valleys and hills, and fished in its many streams and rivers. The first long hunters entered the area before 1770 they began to mark and name the different areas. Communities began to take shape. By 1789, religion by the Presbyterians began to develop and the Liberty Meeting House was begun. That building was erected in what is now the Old Liberty Cemetery. The name Centerville was used because it was thought that the confluence of two streams of the Rolling Fork was the geographical center of the state.

In 1803 a family by the name of Bradford came to the area from Pennsylvania. They came, as others, to find a new way of life, to find their fortunes, and they were attracted to the abundant water supply in the area. That is where our story of Bradfordsville begins.

SECTION I: Beginning of the Town

Once the beginnings of a town took shape, the citizens turned their attention to building a church. In 1789 a meeting was called, in what is now Bradfordsville, to decide where to locate the Presbyterian Church. Those on the community were: James McBride, Samuel McElroy, James McElroy, John Simpson, John McMurry, James Wilson, John McElroy, and Reverend Thomas Cleland, Sr. They decided to build on Hardin's Creek in what is now Lebanon, in the area where the Lebanon City Hall stands in 2018.

1813 the Liberty Meeting House Presbyterian Church was formed, using the crude log building which had been simply called The Liberty Meeting House which stood where the Old Liberty Cemetery was later established. Nathan N. Hall was the first pastor. The church had blacks and whites worshiping together, which was unusual in those days. After the Civil War, the whites left the Liberty Meeting House and established a church in Bradfordsville where the Baptists and Presbyterians shared the Union Church for many years. The Liberty Meeting House was moved down the hill, several yards from its first site. It continued to serve its black members. The area below the hill became the burial place for the blacks, and the ground on top of the hill became the graveyard for the whites in the community. It was at this time the graveyard became known as the Old Liberty Cemetery.

Around 1803, Adam Bradford and his family, being part of the Westward Movement of pioneers, traveled from Pennsylvania to Bradfordsville. The town was in its earliest growth and the Bradfords liked what they saw. The abundant water supply was most pleasant to them. They built a log home on the banks of the North Rolling Fork River. The river had been so named in 1774 by Henry Coppage as it seemed not to run as other rivers do, but instead it appeared to roll along the ledges and rocks, and a high amount of elevation sped the waters along. The process to get to Louisville took around 2 weeks. After one of these trips, Adam and his son, Peter, said that would be their last trip, they would have their own mill before time to go again, which they did.

The Bradford house was more like a cabin type house across the river from where the community lay. Their mill was probably on the other side of the North Rolling Fork. As the community grew, it began to be called Bradford's Mill instead of Centerville. By 1834, the community had grown so much that a post office was established. Instead of calling it Bradford's Mill or Centerville, they chose to name the post office Bradfordsville.

Leadership in the community began to take shape and in 1836 a group of founders decided to approach the Kentucky General Assembly and petition to be certified as a City. Dr. Rose, who had left the East to overcome bankruptcy, drew a map of how the community looked and as to how it should continue to grow. His plan was symmetrical with 3 main roads and cross roads intersecting those main roads. There was also a road bed in the river itself, which was useful during the summer and fall when the water levels were low. Several men went to Frankfort to seek the title for the town, and on January 30, 1836, the state of Kentucky granted city status to Bradfordsville. Those listed by the state of Kentucky as trustees of the town were: Micajah Malone, William M. Chelf, William F. Scanland, James Bradford (brother to Adam), and Joseph Rose. One can imagine the celebration when those men returned from Frankfort with the good news.

The vision of what they wanted for their town was very important because they planned for a large business and residential area to serve all the valleys of the settlers up all the creeks on North Fork, South Fork, and the creeks along the way toward Taylor County (which was Green County at that time), and toward Calvary and Lebanon. The present Riverview Drive was the Main Street. Businesses were along both sides of the street with sidewalks and curbs made of rock. Even now, if you dig about 10 feet from the present road you will find these rocks that marked the edge of the road. The street was very broad so to allow wagons and horses to negotiate along the business area. A fine hotel, blacksmith shop, flour mill, hat factory (the first factory in the county), tannery shop, saw mill, broom factory, wool or carding business, grist mill, livery stable, tavern, shoe shop, county store and more were to be found on the busy Main Street of this growing community.

Mill much like the Bradford's Mill

SECTION II: CIVIL WAR

By 1860 the Bradfordsville town population had increased to around 200. The county area that depended on Bradfordsville businesses was growing steadily. As the Civil War began, Bradfordsville was besieged with difficulties as most of the country was experiencing the same. Major Levin Drye, from Casey County, was a Union soldier. Near the end of the war Major Drye became injured. Union military leaders, knowing he was an important leader, and wanting to accommodate him while he recuperated placed him in Bradfordsville in charge of a union troop known as the invalid troop. Bradfordsville had fared well not to have had great loss during the war but toward the end of the war things took a change. William Clark Quantill had been a guerilla soldier of the Confederacy in Missouri and Kansas. He had caused much damage as he murdered and pillaged the area unmercifully. With 400 soldiers at his command thousands were murdered. In one instance, in Lawrence, Kansas, nearly 400 were killed in one town alone. On Jan 1, 1865, he entered Kentucky—some say he knew the war was over and he was going to surrender, and others say he was on his way to assassinate President Lincoln. Whatever his goals, he worked his way toward Central Kentucky.

By the end of January, Quantrill made a trip through New Market and on toward Bradfordsville, and continued on to Hustonville. He surveyed the area looking for volunteers and resources. While in Hustonville, one of his men, while trying to get fresh horses, murdered a Union soldier. The entire area became inflamed to end this before it got worse. Burning with anger, the men of the community gave chase, determined to bring the murderous gang to their end. Quantrill was accompanied by around 40 including Sue Mundy and Frank James whose older brother, Jesse James, had at this time been sent to Texas. The chase led Quantrill through a route toward Danville, and on toward Lebanon, and toward Nelson County where they found sympathizers and were considered much as Rock stars are today.

Quantrill heard of a supply wagon that would be going through New Market at the beginning of February, so he planned a second rally through the area. At this second time many of Quantrill's men were killed as were many of the Union soldiers. Quantrill captured some of the Union soldiers and headed toward Bradfordsville. At the toll gate house, where Mannsville Road intercepts Highway 49, they tired of trying to prevent the hostages from escaping, and killed them just as Major Drye with his forces came into action. Major Drye chased after Quantrill's forces as they endeavored to escape in Bradfordsville. The community was unaware of what was happening as Quantrill's men needing horses entered the town. The hotel began to ring its bell atop the structure to warn the people. In retaliation for the early warning, Quantrill's forces began to burn and pillage the community, destroying many structures.

There was much pillage and robbery, but no indication that anyone was killed in the melee. Doctor Fleece was awaiting a patient in the old house across the street where Alvin and Laura Wren now live. The doctor's fine horse was taken and a nag was left in its place. That was just one of the many such happenings on that horrible day. The town lay burning that afternoon, with over half of the businesses in ruin, even the cabin home of the Bradfords across the river was destroyed. Quantrill's men were chased toward Hustonville route and were gone, but Bradfordsville was a disaster. Dr. Perry Rose, a very deaf man, was going to help a patient and became the only Bradfordsville casualty as he did not hear the Union forces call him to halt and he continued to go forward.

The town was in so much devastation, but once the shock was over the spirit of the Bradfordsvillians kicked in. They decided to relocate the business area two streets over to what we now call Main Street because cleanup would be ongoing and necessary to clear away all the burn and destruction of the former Main Street. (That burned and destroyed Main Street is now Riverview Drive).

Calvary Soldiers

SECTION III: Reconstruction

The faith of the Bradfordsvillians sustained them through the trials of the Civil War. From its beginning, churches had served as a vital lifeline for the community. The Christian Congregational Church opened here in 1833. The Methodist was mentioned in the Quarterly Conference Board on March 7, 1840. The Baptist and the Presbyterians shared the same building in 1880. (This was possibly the same building where the Masonic Lodge was located in 1877). In 1910, on Joner Creek, the Latter Day Saints of Bradfordsville was first to sustain a worship group in the state of Kentucky. They later built a church on Central Avenue in Bradfordsville.

Nor did the war interfere with the continuation of the Grand Lodge, Masonic Lodge #136, which came to Bradfordsville on August 28, 1844. John H. Tucker was first Master, and Dr. John F. Fleece was first Senior Warden.

In 1865, after the war, things began to go back to normal. There was an upsurge of growth in the community. The Bradford family, whose house had been destroyed by Quantrill's group, began to build a replacement. When completed, their house was a beautiful mansion across the river from town.

In 1866, Bradfordsville Home College began, being fully accredited with the state of Kentucky. There were many prestigious faculty and staff members including Governor Augustus O. Stanley who taught Greek and Latin. The school was incorporated January 28, 1866 and had many graduates. The school ended before 1900. The building was taken down and the bricks were reused in constructing the Rolling Fork Bank near the present intersection of Highways 337 and 49.

In 1875, Baker Terhune built a large mill complex that housed the Bradfordsville Roller Mills. The fine flour and meal produced here were Lafayette and Alpine Snow Flours. They were notable for their specialty grinding.

The Rice Bradford House, a large house on the corner of Third Street and Riverview Drive, became a private school with Annie Newcomb being the teacher.

The Bradfordsville overall factory, that operated 24 hours a day, located on Central Avenue behind present Baptist Church. This complex paid good wages and produced Elk Brand Overalls. This factory was one of the reasons that electricity came early in 1909 to the community.

Bradfordsville in about 1910. The large white building was the Bradfordsville Independent School. It sat on a hill looking down on the town.

In 1900, Bradfordsville Independent Schools built a large school on the hill that served the area. A high school was added in 1912. In 1924, the school district was given over to Marion County and a large stone building, for both high school and elementary, was built.

In 1911, Don Drye, Sr., son of Major Levin Drye, and his partner, Edgar Lewis, built a huge department store which was 3 floors, counting the Kuloff basement restaurant. The store slogan was "from the cradle to the grave" indicating they covered everything needed in a lifetime. It was during this time that Bradfordsville had several businesses including a 3 story Milburn Opera house with a movie theater, pool hall and car sales area, two hotels—the Surber and the Purdy hotels, Shugars & Dinwiddle Drugstore, livery stable, Rolling Fork Bank, D. O. Burke's Carpenter and Butcher Shop, Oatley Burke's Store, two businesses with elevators, Powell Building, and many other businesses and commerce that was the envy of any town its size.

Population continued to grow: 301 in 1900 and to 330 by 1910. There were dips but the numbers rose to their peak in 1960 with 387. The large population of rural people, who used the businesses and depended on them, made prosperity for all.

SECTION IV: Bradfordsville School Strike

As time passed, traveling proved to be easier as automobiles became affordable and available to the average American. No longer was it necessary to purchase goods within horse-driven distance and people enjoyed the expansion of their shopping experience. World War I and World War II affected the national population, including rural areas and small towns. The Depression Era that began in 1929 and stretched through the 30s and 40s strained the economy of the nation, reaching deep into the pockets of Americans. Bradfordsvillians were not exempted. Many graduates from Bradfordsville moved away to find good paying jobs in larger towns and other vicinities. During the years, several fires swept through the small town of Bradfordsville, and not having a local fire department, destroyed fine homes and businesses. It became harder and harder for citizens to rebuild. Thus, the churches and the school became the unifying institutions for the community. Sadly, the death toll began to sound for one. Unbelievably, it was Religion ringing the bell.

In order to explain the history of our schools, the following has been lifted randomly but with similar wording, from <u>A Summation of the Bradfordsville School Case</u> by Jesse K. Lewis, the lawyer hired by Rawlings.

Under the school program adopted in 1937, high school centers were established at Bradfordsville in the eastern part of

Marion County, and St. Charles located in the western part. At this time, Bradfordsville had the largest high school enrollment outside the independent high school in Lebanon, the county seat. The population of the western end and the population in the eastern end were approximately the same.

An analysis must include the Marion County Board of Education was made up of a Catholic superintendent, two Catholic members, two Protestant members—one of whom was A. C. Glasscock, a Baptist and chairman of the Board. From early on, it was evident that Glasscock did not want to lend support to the Bradfordsville School in any way. Therefore, he lent his support, and vote, to the Catholic majority on the board.

Catholic nuns were teaching in the public schools in the western section. This amounted to the government officials of Kentucky hiring the Catholic Church through its nuns to teach in public schools. It also supported the fact that the Catholic hierarchy—not the laymen—had offered Catholic votes to public officials to bring about this violation with impunity of the Constitution and the laws of Kentucky.

Around 1945, the Catholic superintendent, Hugh Spalding, and the Catholic controlled Board of Education began to deviate from the policy and program of the State Department of Education of Kentucky in building up the western end schools. One reason being there were some fifty Catholic high school students living nearer Bradfordsville than they did to the St. Charles High School where the nuns taught. Because of this religious factor the board adopted the policy of giving the students a choice of where they wanted to go to school, and of course, this was done so that the Catholic children could be taught by Catholic nuns. This was in violation of Kentucky law.

About this time a Catholic priest proposed that he should come to the grade school attended by both Protestants and Catholics alike and teach the Catholic catechism. Of course, this aroused the opposition of the Protestants, and the plan fell through. The Catholics then built a grade school only two miles from this one public school and installed nuns as teachers, transferring the Catholic children from the grade school to this Catholic school. The county board then put on another bus at public expense in order to transport the Catholic students to this new school, which the county had rented from the Catholic Church.

During this time, the county board was expending large sums of public funds to equip the St. Charles High School. The board built a new agriculture shop building, purchased new equipment, and did everything to make that school more attractive to the farm boys and girls, including the teaching of home economics and commercial courses.

At the same time, the county board discontinued vocational agriculture and home economic classes at Bradfordsville, and refused to offer commercial courses. The citizens of Bradfordsville came to realize that the county board had set out to destroy the Bradfordsville School.

During this period of time the board had made capital outlay expenditures of approximately $650,000. However, the only money spent at Bradfordsville was to convert the agricultural workroom into a cafeteria. Of the capital outlay of expenditures, $100,000 was for new grounds and new equipment, $40,000 was for improvements of the western end schools, and approximately $60,000 for new sites and additions to old sites. A former board member testified, "We spend all our time voting this for St. Charles and this for Glasscock schools, and when we get through there is nothing left for Bradfordsville."

In 1954, the county board closed the Bradfordsville High School. In response, Rev. J. C. Rawlings, of Bradfordsville, filed suit against the State Superintendent of Public Instruction and six county boards of education in Kentucky, wherein he challenged the right of Catholic nuns to teach in public schools and requested that Bradfordsville High School be reopened again. The parents of the Bradfordsville students, wanting to publicize the ruthless discrimination the Marion County Board of Education had applied to Bradfordsville, chose to strike, refusing to send their children to school until the Bradfordsville High School was restored. The strike extended through the school term of 1954-55. By the fall of '55, the crucial matter had not been resolved. Some students reluctantly gave in and attended Lebanon High School.

Jesse Purdy

The community bought a school bus and Matt Wiser was designated the driver. The second year one of the students, Jesse Purdy, drove the bus. This means of transportation afforded several students a way to attend high school in Hustonville, Nelson County, Kentucky. Some students chose to provide their own transportation and attend school in other counties. Some of the students dropped out of school...some married...some entered the workplace without the benefit of a high school education. That fall of 1955, the elementary students began their studies in the Bradfordsville Elementary School. The lawsuit lay dormant somewhere in the halls of the Justice System.

The decision made in the case on June 22, 1956, by the Kentucky Court of Appeals declared the Marion County Board of Education, in closing the Bradfordsville School in 1954, and ordering its students to attend school in Lebanon, acted arbitrarily, and in excess of its lawful powers.

The Court of Appeals ordered the Marion County School Board to (1) Stop violating the State laws that prohibits sectarian books and literature of the Roman Catholic Church to be distributed in public schools. (2) Stop placing sectarian periodicals in and about the libraries of the public schools. (3) Stop spending public school funds for religious purposes. (4) Maintain school-bus runs on Catholic holidays that are not also legal state or national holidays.

The Court added:

"It seems to us that the entire county system of schools should be reorganized so as to produce substantial equality for the entire county and to abolish sectarianism in all parts thereof."

The Marion County Board of Education was also ordered to establish one centrally located union high school for the entire county, or reopen the Bradfordsville High School. In time, the board decided on establishing the one centrally located high school on the outskirts of Lebanon.

The Court's decision was a sweeping condemnation of biased handling of school facilities by the Marion County Board of Education, and constituted a new cornerstone in the structure of freedom in public schools. The citizens of Bradfordsville area had waged a valiant fight to regain their high school. Their battle for justice set a tone to which all the county is now attuned. It happened by the strength, unity, diligence, and courage of Bradfordsvillians.

Dr. Martin Luther King Jr. understood the power of the past. He once said, "We are not makers of history. We are made by history." So it is that Bradfordsvillians have been made by their history. In their veins flow a continuation of the courage of their ancestors who braved the journey into the Kentucky wilderness, to clear the land, build their homes, establish towns, institute laws, build schools and churches, and attain a good life for themselves and others who followed.

A Bradfordsvillian is a person who enjoys the beauty of the knobs, meadows, rivers and streams—all of which offer contentment to the heart. A Bradfordsvillian finds comradeship in friendly and helpful neighbors. A Bradfordsvillian is a faithful member of the church of his/her choice. A Bradfordsvillian will always be proud to be called just that....a BRADFORDSVILLIAN.

SHENANIGANS

In the sweetness of friendship let there be laughter and sharing of pleasure. For in the dew of little things the heart finds its morning and is refreshed.

Khalil Gibran

CLYDE WILSON'S FLAGRANT SON

He was supposed to be a girl. His father's niece, Nellie Spalding, had already picked out his name: Emma Nell. On that October day, 1936, when he entered the world at Baute Hospital in Lebanon, it was obvious another name needed to be chosen. Dear Nellie didn't give up and so she offered: Bobby Lee Wilson. That was accepted until "Miss" Edith, his mother, decided he needed a name better suited to carry him though manhood, and she changed the name to Robert Lee Wilson. As time passed he was stuck with "Bobby" until his antics and his name collided and then he gained the short and easier name to exclaim, and that was "Bob"!

Ed Wilson, Bob Wilson around 1942

He was a born leader and his slightly older brother, Ed, obliged him by becoming his follower. If Ed didn't follow, he at least admired his antics, and that helped fuel Bob's energetic and mischievous spirit. He was the youngest of the Wilson brood with three older brothers and two older sisters, all of whom were studious, mannerly, and perfectly behaved. And then came Bob!

Right next door to the Wilson's lived other nice neighbors.

They were Mr. Don Drye, Senior, and "Miss" Edna, his wife. (In the '40s, older married ladies were referred to as "Miss".) Miss Edna had a chicken lot between their house and the Wilson's. Bob and Ed had an abundant supply of finger firecrackers; the adjective "finger" describing perfectly the size and shape of the firecrackers. Chickens loved to chase after corn tossed to them, and sometimes they had difficulty distinguishing corn from firecrackers. Bob and Ed found it great fun lighting a small firecracker, throwing it into the chicken lot, and watching the hens, cackling, chase it down, grab it up, and "BANG," off went their heads.

They tried it several times and decided too many headless chickens might cause suspicion that could lead to them, and so, reluctantly, they discontinued their sport. Miss Edna probably thought some strange varmint was getting into her chicken lot and killing her chickens in an odd manner. Whatever her thoughts, she didn't pursue them.

At a young age, Bob became a dead shot with a single shot twenty-two caliber rifle. Later, in high school, he earned his way to the State Junior Conservation Rifle Contest, but back to our story. In those days, electric lines went through blue/green glass insulators, and those pretty little things sitting up high were tempting little targets to a kid with a rifle. So many were shot out of the lines at Bradfordsville that the electric company sent investigators to find the culprit. When the investigators arrived at the Wilson home, they saw young Bob running into the barn, so they followed. They gave the frightened boy a lecture about the cost of those insulators and the

cost of installing them. Their authoritarian manner and stern lecture impressed Bob. Those pretty blue-green insulators stayed intact from then on.

Mr. and Mrs. Drye had a pretty little granddaughter, Suzanne Cundiff. Suzanne was a bit younger than the Wilson boys. The Cundiffs were visiting the Dryes and Suzanne's mother had dressed her for church. Her blond hair was perfectly curled with a pretty ribbon attached. Her dress was white, starched, and freshly ironed. She went out to play in the yard while her folks dressed.

The vision of that cute little girl, dressed in starched white, happily playing was too much prettiness for Ed and Bob. So they turned the water hose on her. One can imagine Mrs. Cundiff's dismay when Suzanne came crying, dripping wet, into the house.

She immediately started out the door to give those young monsters a sound whipping. Miss Edna stopped her. "Now, Alene," Miss Edna admonished, "You can't whip the neighbors' children!" Mrs. Cundiff gave it a second thought, and the Wilson boys got off free one more time!

On the upper side of the Wilsons lived an older widow, Miss Nanny Burke. Miss Nanny was a very proper older lady who had been left financially secure by her late husband. She dressed the part, always wearing a hat to church, and walking with a stiff back and her head held high. Miss Nanny prided herself on how well she could drive. She drove a 1938 Buick which she always parked in front of her house, facing upper part of town called Fairview. When she needed to go someplace, she backed down the street, backed into the Wilson driveway, and then would turn toward downtown.

Mr. Clyde Wilson, (Bob's father) had cut down a tree next to their drive and a large stump was left in place. Bob was standing in their front yard one day when Miss Nanny came backing down the street.

She rolled down her window and asked, "Am I doing alright, Bob?" Bob eyed the stump directly behind her car, and he yelled, "You're doing fine, Miss Nanner. Come on back!"

She threw it into reverse again, pressed down on the pedal, and backed that 1938 Buick to the top of the stump. At that, she threw the gears into drive and pressed down on the accelerator.

The engine roared but the differential sat firmly balanced on the stump with the wheels spinning on both sides. The car was going no place.

Miss Nanny got out and saw the situation for what it was. Bob went running. Miss Nanny then knocked on the Wilson's door to get Mr. Clyde's assistance. Mr. Clyde had to get the car jack, jack up the car and push it off the stump.

She got inside the car and went on her way. Bob finally had to appear and, yes, his dad "laid into him." Bob received his punishment with his usual manner. He thought seeing Miss Nanny's car running up that stump and those wheels spinning in air was worth any spanking Mr. Clyde could dish out!

A sixteenth birthday was always a most welcome day in a teenager's life. It meant finally being able to legally drive a car, not that in the '50's most of us were not driving cars by our twelfth year. Bradfordsville sat in the middle of farm land and young people found themselves early on behind the driver's wheel of their parents' tractor and even the farm trucks. Illegal driving was not a big deal, but still it was gratifying at the age of sixteen to become the proud owner of a driver's license.

One evening the Wilsons were preparing to eat their dinner. (Everyone else in Bradfordsville called it supper, but to the Wilsons the evening meal was dinner.) It was discovered the meal was lacking bread and Bob volunteered to drive to the store to pick up a loaf. Of course, Bob took the scenic route and drove to the First Iron Bridge before turning around.

Just as he turned his dad's '52 Plymouth around, Jimmy Wooley crossed the bridge in his dad's '52 slant-back Chevrolet. Bob flagged him down. "Wanta race?" he asked. "Sure," Jimmy answered, and the race was on.

Jimmy was in the right lane and Bob was in the left passing lane. They were fast approaching the sharp curve in front of Ben Dock Rake's house. Ben Dock was sitting on his front porch. Bob was determined to get ahead of Jimmy, and Jimmy seeing the curve, and knowing Bob, began to slow down to let Bob ahead. Too late! Bob entered the curve going at top speed. His car left the road on the right side, turned up on two wheels. Bob over adjusted and veered to the left side, taking the Rake's mailbox and some fence planks with him. Back again to the right side before he finally gained control and eased back onto the highway. Jimmy breezed by, not even waving his hand. Ben Dock Rakes saw it all from his front porch.

Bob drove home with the bread. Getting out, he surveyed the car. It looked OK and so he nonchalantly entered the house, delivered the bread, and sat down to eat, all the while waiting for the phone to ring. But surprisingly, it never rang.

The next day the Wilson family departed for their jobs: Mr. Clyde started his mail route; Miss Edith headed to school to teach her piano classes, and Bob and Ed gathered their books for school. All went well until Mr. Clyde reached Ben Dock's mailbox, which was bent out of shape, and Ben Dock was mending his fence.

"Looks like someone took out your mail box and went through your fence," Mr. Clyde remarked.

"Yep," answered Mr. Rakes.

"Know who it was?" asked Mr. Clyde.

"Yep," said Mr. Rakes.

"Well, who was it?"

"Your boy," answered Mr. Rakes.

As one might expect, Bob had to buy some planks with his money made from mowing yards. He had to help repair the damage. Luckily, the car wasn't hurt.

When Ben Dock later told the story he recalled, "All I could see was the underside of a car as it went around the curve on just its two wheels!"

Someone with Higher Power must have been watching over Bob Wilson.

Jeannette Wooley & Bob Wilson married in 2008

The Morgesons

There were four children still at home during the time of our story. They were Perry, Buster, Frances, and Clarence. Mr. Les Morgeson was our school's janitor. He was a gentle, kind man and all of us loved him.

Mrs. Lora Morgeson was the town's telephone operator. A switch board sat in their living room and communication was achieved by customers turning their telephone cranks a certain number of rings, some short and some long. There were party lines. All the folks sharing a line could hear the rings and many would pick up their phones to listen in on their neighbors' conversations. Picking up your phone sounded a click. Hearing a click meant someone was listening to what was being said, but their identification would remain a mystery.

Sometimes Mrs. Morgeson needed to run an errand and she would leave a child in charge of the switchboard. If you happened to be visiting at such a time, a whole different style of entertainment was opened to you. It was such fun to call Harmon's grocery and ask about a tobacco product. The conversation would go something like this:

"Do you have Prince Albert in a can?"

"Yes, we do."

"You'd better let him out before he smothers."

Then you could call a busy housewife and ask, "Is your refrigerator running?"

"Why, yes, it is."

"You had better hurry and try to catch it!"

Such fun in the town! One couldn't have fun like that on a farm.

Mr. Morgeson's school keys offered another form of entertainment. Of course, they had to be sneaked out which required some timing and planning. Remember when "there is a will, there is always a way"!

One sleepy Sunday afternoon, Bob went down to visit Clarence. Access to the keys was gained and the two boys headed over to the school to shoot a few shots of basketball in the gym. Bob soon became bored with that game and suggested they go up to the science lab where he could demonstrate to younger Clarence some amazing science stuff. Clarence was all for the idea and up to the science lab they went!

The lab was a typical science work place. It had sinks, chemicals, testing tubes, and other chemistry equipment. Bob decided to go into the back room and get some sodium and a beaker. After setting the beaker over the sink's drain, he poured

some water into it. He then took out his knife and cut off a piece of sodium about 1 inch diameter and dropped it into the beaker. The mixture started sparkling with fire flying and swirling around the beaker.

A little is never enough for Bob and so he added more water to it. The water hit the mixture and the beaker exploded. Glass flew all over the room embedding in everything it hit. Smoke went up and then down into the drain. After the smoke went as far into the drain as it could go, a mushroom cloud emerged, growing larger and larger as it rose toward the ceiling. Bob and Clarence had hit the floor at the time of the explosion. There above them the cloud was spreading out, covering an area about four feet diameter with yellow coating.

Principal, B.H. Crowe

The shocked boys stared at the destruction. Broken glass slivers were everywhere. Observing the huge yellow circle above helped determine their decision to quickly leave. And so they did, locking the doors behind them.

On Monday morning, the school was abuzz about the disastrous discovery in the science lab. Mr. Crowe, the principal, made rounds trying to see if he could scare the guilty person, or persons, into owning up to their making the mess. No one admitted anything. When he finally reached Bob's room, his angry glare focused on Bob. He said, "I don't know who did it, but I would bet anything that Bob Wilson had something to do with it!"

Bob innocently shrugged his shoulders, and held his hands out with their palms up, as if to say, "Who? Not me."

Buster was a Jokester

All the Morgeson's enjoyed pranks and jokes, but Buster was perhaps the best at it. One day when several visitors were sitting around the room, unknown to them, Buster had previously placed

a big hunk of pumpkin pie filling on the edge of his shoe's sole. Sitting with the visitors, Buster crossed his legs, as men do, with the right "pumpkined" shoe resting on his left thigh. In short time, one of the guests said, "Buster, you've got something on your shoe. You've stepped in something."

Buster looked at the gooey hunk hanging to his shoe. He then took his finger and raked off a fair amount, raised it to his nose, then, to his lips. To everyone's horror, he took a bite. "Yep," he said, smacking his lips, "it's dog sh*t."

Perry and the Hotdogs

Sometimes, it's the mind's visual that gives humor to a story. Thus, it was with young Perry Morgeson and the hotdogs.

Down on Main Street in the basement of Drye's Department store was a sandwich shop that teenagers used for a hangout. They sometimes danced there to the disdain of the Baptists in town.

Two older boys had been hired to clean the shop on certain days after the facility closed. Young Perry, about eight years old, yearned to get inside and see what to him was a mysterious place. Knowing fancy food was served inside made it all the more desirable for a youngster to explore.

Perry kept knocking on the door but the boys inside had been directed to not let anyone in while they cleaned. Perry was persistent with his knocking and finally the cleaners decided that a little kid like that could do no harm and they opened the door. Wonder of wonders, the place could have been an early Disney Land to young Perry's eyes. There against the wall was a refrigerated box that held the delicious ingredients from which sandwiches were made.

While the older boys were busy sweeping, Perry peered into the box and spied some hotdogs. Temptation overcame him, and intending to grab one hotdog, he quickly reached into the container for the object of his desire. Now he was not aware that in those times hot dogs were not manufactured singularly but in strings attached to each other, end to end.

He grabbed a hotdog and ran for the door. The older boys looked up and couldn't believe their eyes. There went Perry out the door with a long string of hotdogs flying behind him! What a comical sight.

Perry was as surprised as they were when he found his loot was a string of hotdogs instead of one. In rare cases such as this, crime does pay.

The Mysterious Leaf

Biology 101 always contained a unit on the study of leaves. Bradfordsville students were mostly familiar with different types of trees in the woods where they loved to play, and where many loved to hunt. It was a simple joke to them to actually have a unit on leaves and their identifications. Since it was an easy class to sit through, the students welcomed the relief from more strenuous assignments.

One fall in 1953, the class proved stressful, not to the class, but to the teacher. Marion County School Board had assigned Paul Mills from Lebanon to teach science in the Bradfordsville High School. Students were suspicious that assignment might have had something to do with Mr. Mill's breath. Sometimes it smelled of spirits. Nevertheless, Mr. Mills proved to adequately fill the job's requirements and science was taught. Then came the unit on leaves.

Mr. Mills came up with an ingenious lesson plan. Each student was to bring in a leaf; it would be identified, and then displayed on a poster board. That was easy enough. All a student had to do was grab a leaf while running for the school bus and, ding, the assignment was half done.

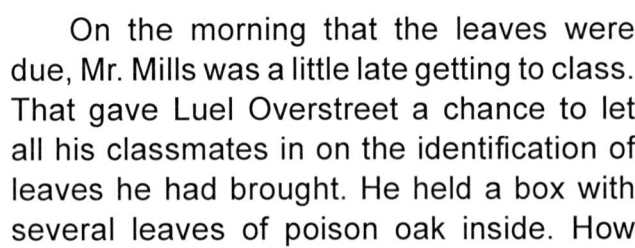

On the morning that the leaves were due, Mr. Mills was a little late getting to class. That gave Luel Overstreet a chance to let all his classmates in on the identification of leaves he had brought. He held a box with several leaves of poison oak inside. How this was going to "play out" made uneasiness fill each heart beating in that classroom.

Mr. Mills arrived and class began. The colorful fall leaves were pleasing to examine and the discussion of chlorophyll, photosynthesis, osmosis, leaf veins, and different shapes held the interest of the students. Then came time for Luel to display his leaves.

Luel opened his box being careful in the way he held it. Mr. Mills picked up a leafy stem to examine. He was baffled. He wasn't sure what it was. Luel confessed that he didn't know either. For some unknown reason, Mr. Mills smelled the leaves. "Elll," he said in the way he habitually began most of his sentences. "Elll, I think it is some kind of oak." Stifled snickers could almost be heard throughout the room.

The next day a pink Mr. Mills arrived at school. His face, hands, and arms were covered with pink Caladryl. It was almost enough to make a whole classroom of science students feel remorse. Mr. Mills continued his teaching without admonishing anyone. Perhaps he, too, felt guilty that he hadn't been able to identify a simple poison oak leaf. Whatever his reason, he never mentioned how he became pink overnight and the class didn't ask.

A Bird? A Snake? No, It's a Child

The Beards were a lovable farm family that included several children. (If one attended Bradfordsville School that person was officially a Bradfordsvillian and so the Beards can be included here). At the time of this story the children were: Anna Blaine, being the oldest; then, Mary Lou, Sally Carol, Moses, and baby, Sammy. With so many active young minds, it was inevitable that some inventive shenanigans would be construed. They were.

Farms in the '40's and '50's always had a large mailbox beside the main highway. A mailbox had to be big in order to hold the large packages containing needed merchandise for the farm family. It was common for pranksters to put garden snakes, birds, opossums, and such in mailboxes to startle the mailman. The Beard children weren't going to deal with that small stuff, and so it was decided to put baby Sammy in the box.

Knowing the exact time the mailman always delivered, Sammy was placed in the mailbox, on his knees, facing the door. In short time, the mailman pulled up, stopped in front of the box, and arranged the mail that was to be placed inside. He then pulled down the mailbox door and there was a bright eyed baby staring at him! It scared him half to death! He somehow gained control of his senses and retrieved the baby, handing him to the children who had come out of hiding. He mused that he had seen all kinds of creatures which flew or jumped from mailboxes, but this was the first time he found a delightful, bright-eyed baby boy.

IDA BELLE

In earlier times, one room schools dotted the hills and valleys of Marion County. From these rural schools came future doctors, lawyers, teachers, nurses, and others who chose all kinds of work for their life's labor.

Drye School lay between the Rush Branch community and the town of Bradfordsville. One of its students was Ida Belle Marple. She later married Al Evans, reared three strapping sons, and taught for a while in Marion County. In those days she was a keen-minded young girl with a self-determined disposition. Not many things could faze Ida Belle, not then, not ever.

All the grades had finished reciting their lessons at the teacher's desk and it came time to practice spelling. That particular day the teacher went from one to one, asking each to spell a chosen word. When he came to Ida Belle, he asked her to spell twine. Without a pause she loudly proclaimed, "Twee-i-n-e, twine."

"How…?" quizzed the surprised teacher.

"Twee-i-n-e," answered Ida Belle, very certain she had it right.

"Ida Belle, go to the board and write it."

She scooted from her desk, pranced jauntily to the board, picked up the chalk, put its tip to the blackboard, and paused. Standing there for a moment with the chalk posed in air, with the teacher and her classmates waiting in silent wonderment, Ida Belle turned and asked, "How do you make a "twee"?"

My Baby Groundhogs

Alton Evans and Jeanette Wooley were cousins. Their mothers, Ida Belle Evans and Rhoda Wooley were sisters. These two statements form the setting for our next story.

Jeanette Wooley was always an animal lover. That didn't change after she married and moved to her in-laws farm in Mannsville, Kentucky. One day, the tenant on the farm, Ira Followell, brought two orphaned groundhogs to her door. Her heart melted at the sight of the two furry babies.

Because these animals dig burrows in the farm fields, and wheels of tractors sink into the burrows, and horses or mules can break a leg by stepping into them, gives reason to the farmers to shoot groundhogs. Jeanette didn't question how the babies came to be orphans. Killing groundhogs was a rule of farmers that was universally accepted.

She happily adopted the cute little fellows and found a cardboard box for their home. They were adorable, but being so young meant they would require regular bottling.

Jeanette was teaching fourth grade at Mannsville Elementary. Each day she took her furry babies to school, much to the delight of her students. Bottling groundhogs in a classroom was very unusual to witness. In fact, it was so unusual that a reporter from the Campbellsville News-Journal came out to take pictures and do a write-up. The groundhogs become kind of like celebrities. But a dilemma was developing. Groundhogs grow fast which made their cardboard home get smaller and smaller. A new home was needed, but where and what? It became a huge problem.

The problem was solved when Alton Evans dropped by for a visit and Jeanette confided in him about her dilemma.

"That's no problem," Alton assured her, "I have a perfect place for them."

Relief spread over Jeanette as she recalled the chicken lot, out buildings, and chicken coops behind her Aunt Ida Belle's house where Alton had an upstairs apartment.

She happily relinquished her precious babies and away they went with Alton for their new home in Bradfordsville.

Alton Evans

A few weeks later, Jeanette made a visit to the Evan's home, eager to see how her angels were doing.

"Aunt Belle, I would really love to see my groundhogs," Jeanette announced, thinking of what a pleasure it would be.

A distressful look crossed Ida Belle's face. "I'm sorry, Jeanette, you can't."

"Why not?"

"Alton ate them."

Right Out of the Sky

Hillary Coffman was the only barber in Bradfordsville. He was fastidious about his barbering which his customers appreciated. For many years he only charged 25 cents per cut. He lost a few customers, for a short time, when he went up to 50 cents.

Hillary's barber shop was a great hangout for farmers, especially in the winter months when cropping was slow. Here the latest gossip was told, jokes shared, and the arguments over religion could sometimes get hot. Occasionally Hillary would get out his guitar and play some music. The only drawback to getting a haircut at Hillary's was his slowness. It took at least 45 minutes for him to complete one cut. That could amount to a long wait if three or four people were ahead of you. All in all, it was a good place to spend some time with your neighbors.

The shop was a "real" man's place. Birth control "apparel" that came in small round packages could be bought, even little naughty books referred to with a four-letter word were quietly sold. Now, don't take this wrong. Hillary was in reality a fine gentleman and lived an upright citizen's life.

He and his wife had a neat, small home in Bradfordsville. His wife, Helen, always wore a resemblance of a smile and spoke in a gentle manner. She was so proper that she didn't shave her legs. That was a symbol she didn't engage in anything that hinted of sexuality. After all, that hair grew long and black at puberty so it must have something to do with sex, and the appearance of dealing with sex was to be avoided. It is doubtful she knew about the little books at Hillary's shop, but of course, that is only speculation.

Most nights Hillary's place was open until midnight. They didn't travel much as Hillary worked long hours and Helen kept busy with keeping her home spotless.

One of their prized possessions was a new 1948, two-door, blue Plymouth coupe. Hillary had bought it just after the war. There were few miles on the odometer because they seldom traveled. But one Sunday, they decided to take a leisurely ride over to Liberty, Kentucky, about twenty miles away. There lay a range of higher elevation between Bradfordsville and Liberty.

It was part of a range referred to as Muldraugh's Hills. Going toward Liberty on Highway #49 meant going over these hills on a narrow road with high bluffs on your right, and deep valleys to your left.

Hillary was easily mastering the curves and bends when suddenly a 400 pound wild hog lost its footing on the bluff above and fell twenty feet onto their beautiful car. It is hard to imagine the sound of that sudden loud crash when that 400 pound hog hit the windshield and hood of their blue Plymouth. The car was totally destroyed. The hood was mashed into the motor, the windshield became non-existent, and the car lost any power to move.

Running over animals is a common accident that happens in central Kentucky. People always feel sadness when an unexpected animal dashes in front of their vehicle. A rabbit, a chicken, a dog, a cat, or something similar can be expected, but a wild hog! And through the top of your car!

That day, the quiet life of the Coffman's crashed with the hog. Afterwards, they did regain their normal routines, but if they ever traveled to Liberty again they probably took another route.

Long Names

Before birth certifications became the required legal record of children's births, families wrote such information in the Family Bible. Those Bibles were treasured by families and they were carefully passed from one generation to the next.

At the end of Bradfordsville lived Tynt Brown. His sister, Ada Brown Marple, lived around the corner on Church Street. Their parents were Lafe and Ellen Brown. Several members of the Brown family were thought to be a little peculiar. They were apt to be unusually "set in their ways." They were very prideful. Sometimes they were short-tempered, easily offended. But, mostly, they were extremely intelligent.

Perhaps their peculiarities could be traced back to their father, and to his father. The Family Bible could be used as evidence that they were a little odd, especially in the way they named their children. Lafe Brown's father, Alexander, named him, Archibald Horaticus Marcus LaFayette Brown. He was soon called Lafe.

Lafe and Ellen

Lafe Brown's first child was a baby girl. Perhaps Lafe decided she would be first and last because he named her Maggie Lucinda Zero. (Years later, her daughter vowed the name was "Zero" because she had seen the names in the Family Bible). After Maggie, another girl was born. Choosing a name for her proved to be difficult because neighbor women up and down the creek where they lived had expressed a desire that one of the child's names be their own. The problem was solved by naming the child, Ada Minnie Willie Ellen Lottie Lee Brown. A little boy was next born and Lafe called the baby Aesop. Sadly that child died and it was never mentioned again except to be named on the census. Finally, another son was born and he was named Alexander Tynte. The last child was Thetis Kincaid Coppage McCrosky.

These children grew into adulthood and then they were: Maggie, Ada Lee, Tynte, and Thetis.

Judgement is left to the reader as to the choice of "odd" in describing the Browns. Could there have been a better word?

Do You Remember Me?

Jimmy Wooley and Frances Morgeson married back in 1956 when she was just finishing high school. They were the kind of sweethearts that other teenagers admired. Their relationship seemed to be one "made in heaven." But like so many marriages theirs did not last through the "happily ever after" stage, and after several years and two sons, they divorced and went their separate ways.

Jimmy was not one for school reunions but he finally stopped making excuses for not attending and decided to make his presence at one. It had been a long time since he had seen most of his schoolmates and he wasn't prepared for the physical changes time had given them. He found himself trying to connect faces to memories and getting more and more embarrassed about not being able to recall names.

Patsy Mann Tatum stepped up to him and asked, "Jimmy, do you remember me?" He searched her face and regretfully he admitted he did not. She said, "Well, Jimmy, we dated and were really good friends, and you don't remember me?"

Jimmy shook his head and Patsy waited a few seconds before telling him who she was. They talked for a bit and as she walked away he stood there feeling like a heel for not being able to think of her name. It was at that moment another attractive, fashionable woman walked up to him and asked the same question, "Do you remember me?"

He was still reeling from embarrassment and here he was again in the same dilemma. He searched her features and her short stylish hair with its light reddish tint but nothing was "ringing a bell" in his mind. Finally he said, "I'm so sorry but, no, I don't remember you."

Frances snapped, "D%*#, you! I had TWO kids by you!"

That's when his knees nearly buckled.

That was the last school reunion Jimmy ever attended.

Peeing Over the Farm Gate

WILLIAM WOOLEY

Wooley retires from Lebanon Water Company

William Wooley was the first child born on the Wooley Brothers' farm; thus, he was Charles and Ernest Wooley's first nephew. They loved to tease the little fellow and, of course, much of it was what we call "guy things."

One day they bet the little boy that he couldn't pee over the farm gate. William thought he could. So he prepared himself, looked down, and aimed high. Cutting loose, he peed in his own face!

Bucket of Fire

Parley Bright and his flagrant friend had an ugly prank they loved to play. They went into the barnyard and shoveled the softest cow manure into a bucket. On top of the manure they poured some kerosene. They then chose a neighbor in front of whose door they placed the bucket of soft manure. Next, they lit the kerosene, rang the bell, and ran, hiding behind a bush, or whatever, to watch.

The neighbor would answer the door bell and would spy the flaming bucket. Instinct to quickly extinguish the fire always kicked into the neighbor's brain. Invariably, the impulse was

Parley Bright

to stamp out the fire. Into the bucket would go the foot with force and deep into the soft cow manure would sink that foot, shoe, and pant leg. From the neighbor's mouth would come some obscenity that he, himself, couldn't believe!

With mission accomplished, the gleeful pranksters always ran, never mindful of the mess in which they left their neighbor.

BUICK CLIMBS THE STEPS

As we've said, Miss Nanny Burke prided herself on being a great driver. This incident contradicted her claim. She had been shopping at one of the stores on the main street. Taking off at a rather slow speed, she attempted to change the gears into second on the Christian Church hill. She missed second, and instead, she shifted into reverse!

Immediately, the car started backward at an accelerated speed because Miss Nanny had then hit the gas pedal intending for the brake.

She turned the steering wheel and headed flying backward toward the Drye Department Store. With a loud BANG! BANG! BANG! the Buick climbed the steps and stopped just clear of the glass doors. The loud bangs brought the men out of the barber shop across the street. They stood amazed and stared at the sight.

With a loud roar, Miss Nanny shifted into first and BANG! BANG! BANG! She descended the steps and sped up the church hill leaving all the spectators behind, scratching their heads and laughing.

Where's My Girdle?

Mrs. Nellie Spalding was postmistress at the Bradfordsville Post Office for many years. It was during those times that Miss Nanny ordered a girdle. Days passed and the expected girdle failed to arrive. Miss Nanny began to make daily trips to the post office to inquire about the girdle. Each time, Miss Nellie had to tell her, "No, your package isn't here."

Each day, Miss Nanny grew all the more impatient. After

Post office crew with Miss Nellie in black

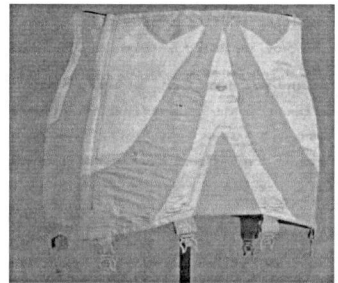

so many days of the "missing" girdle, Miss Nanny became suspicious as to what could be the cause of the girdle's lateness.

Being told one more time that the girdle hadn't arrived, Miss Nanny stared at Miss Nellie's figure. Haughtily, she sneered, "Some people are looking mighty spiffy these days."

Immediately, Miss Nellie grabbed the hem of her dress and raised it to her neck. "Does this look like your girdle?" she inquired of Miss Nanny.

Miss Nanny was shocked seeing the usually proper lady's underwear. She gave a loud huff, spun around and left. Miss Nellie rearranged her dress and went back to sorting mail.

Cruising down the River

As told by Vickie Drye Zerkle

(Many people would say that Dr. David Drye was the favorite son of Bradfordsville. If ever we had any elite in our town, Dr. Drye would be considered one. He came back to his home town to practice medicine. He was an accomplished musician. While the townsfolk would be tapping their feet at a Bluegrass show at the school, David would be at home playing classical music on his baby grand piano. He was a refined gentleman in every sense of the word. That is one of the reasons Vickie's story is so funny.) – Note by Jeanette Wilson

One hot July summer day in the year of 1954, my favorite uncle, Dr. David Drye, decided that we needed to take a canoe trip on the Rolling Fork River. He wanted to take my brother, Donny, and me on this lovely afternoon cruise. He was always interested in us, his nephew and niece, and was always concerned about our wellbeing and keeping us busy in our spare time.

Dr. David Drye

On this particular day he picked us up and we drove to the Old Bradford Place in Bradfordsville. There we put the canoe into the water and started down the river toward the First Iron Bridge. The water was not deep or shallow, just a good level for a canoe trip. However, it was swift, rippling and swirling in certain places. As we approached the First Iron Bridge, Uncle David said, "Now let's be careful and look like we know how to steer a rowboat because there are some people on the bank as we go by watching us." Suddenly the current swirled the canoe around and all our vigorous paddling couldn't control it. That darn boat sailed by those gawking people, going backward! Well, so much for showing off our rowing skills. We provided a comical show to the delight of the amused watchers. It was laughable seeing the refined doctor in such an unrefined position!

As we glided down the river, we neared the area under the cliff by the Drye Farm, and the canoe ran upon a downed log, and completely flipped over! No one was hurt, and we all got in again and proceeded toward the Second Iron Bridge.

Finally, we arrived at the Second Iron Bridge. As we climbed a steep bank, pulling the canoe out, I fell and got a mess of fish hooks in my clothes. Thank goodness, the trip was over, and we were still alive. However, as bad as the trip turned out to be, it will always remain in my mind as one of the most wonderful days of my life!

That Ole Rolling Fork was a center of activity and fun in Bradfordsville.

NOT IN MY WINDOW

Linnie Swiggett

Ray Bright

Linnie Swiggett was perhaps the most independent woman Bradfordsvillians had ever seen. She decided after a few years of marriage, and after the birth of her son, that she wanted a divorce in order to move away and study to be a registered nurse. Her husband granted the divorce and took custody of their small child.

She proceeded to realize her dream. Marriage and motherhood were not for her. She also loved genealogy and helped the Bradfordsville Historical Society with much of their research. She was noted for her brains and, also, for not taking any guff from anyone.

Ray Bright was deaf. It was probably due to a childhood disease such as measles. He helped farmers with their crops, skated at the rink, played cards, and was generally sociable as much as his deafness allowed. But his deafness was a determent to his developing any relationship with a girl. That was probably what fueled his curiosity about women, their lifestyle and their bodies. He satisfied this curiosity by sometimes peeping into their windows.

One time he made the bad mistake of peeping into Linnie's window! Yes, it was bad mostly because she saw him! Quickly, she grabbed her pistol and ran out the door, shooting as she ran. Ray took off, running for his life! Linnie was a good shot! The only thing that saved Ray was Arnold B. Abell's woodpile. He dove behind it and hid as best he could. Linnie planted a few shots into the woodpile and then decided to not pursue the chase. She returned to her house. Ray caught his breath, said a silent prayer, and sneaked home.

No, you better not have messed with Linnie Swiggett!

Skinny Dipping

The boys in town sometimes went skinny dipping in a swimming hole in the North Rolling Fork River behind Pappy Dick Rake's blacksmith shop. They didn't expect any female interference until one day. Tilda Adams, one of the cutest girls in town gave them a surprise visit.

Tilda popped out of the bushes and grabbed their clothes. "Don't do that," yelled the boys. She giggled, enjoying a new found way of getting their attention.

"I think I'll just take these clothes and toss them someplace," she teased.

Parley said, "Give us back our clothes or I'm coming after them."

"You wouldn't do that," Tilda said with a hint of doubt in her voice.

"Oh, yes, I would," said Parley, as he started climbing out of the water.

Tilda screamed, dropped the clothes, and ran.

It was rumored that Parley was perhaps the only teenage boy there that day who had no need to feel shame in appearing nude. You know what I mean.

Tilda Adams

Daring Willard Rakes

Near the Second Iron Bridge there is a knob named Buzzard Knob. It derived its name from the numerous turkey buzzards that make its top their home. To most people they are disgusting  birds because carrion makes up their diet. They find carrion in recent roadkill or from any small, dead critter. Turkey buzzards have a wing span of 63 to 72 inches making them very large creatures.

Buzzards are not very clean by human standards. For instance, they often defecate on their own legs using the evaporation of the water in the feces and urine to cool themselves. This causes uric acid to stain their legs. Their primary form of defense is regurgitating semi-digested meat, a foul-smelling substance. This substance will burn a person's face, if it ever comes in contact with a face.

Willard Rakes was with a group of Bradfordsville boys who hiked to the top of Buzzard Knob one summer afternoon. From its height they looked out over the valley where Bradfordsville lay, and they could see the Rolling Fork River winding through the farm land. Everything was beautiful except for the buzzard droppings all around. Boys

Willard at work

will be curious even in the vicinity of filth. What really caught their attention was the cave where some of the buzzards made their home. They wondered if there could be a buzzard inside.

A discussion went back and forth among them. Willard figured that the discussion was a waste of time. He thought if you really wanted to know something it would require action and not a lot of talking. He announced, "I'm going in after them!"

Without a moment of hesitation, Willard entered the cave.

An eerie silence fell over the shocked boys. They wondered if they should have tried to stop him Then again, it was going to be exciting to see what would emerge from the cave. They waited. Soon there was the sound of a lot of flapping, hissing, and a lot of commotion. Out came Willard dragging a huge, regurgitating buzzard with flapping wings that span five or six feet. Those flapping wings spread out as far as some of the boys were tall.

Willard had quite a wrestle getting that huge buzzard out of that cave! Everyone was amazed and had witnessed something they would never forget. To Willard, it wasn't a big deal. If you want to know something, you go for it. Yes, there was a buzzard in that cave.

Later that summer, for fun Willard jumped into the Rolling Fork River from the top of the Second Iron Bridge. He survived! He made a name for himself as being the most daring and entertaining young man his friends had ever seen.

Second Iron Bridge

Pets

In the early 1900's, Ben Wooley had a parrot that sat in a tree and cursed.

Sometime in the 1940's and 1950's, Bob Crews had a pet fox.

The Wooley kids had a Shepherd dog, Jack, that could climb ladders to the roofs of outbuildings but had to be carried down.

Oscar Spalding had a cat named Mousey, who would on command stuff a ball into a shoe. Mousey would fuss about it but always carried through with the task, even stuffing it tighter if at first Oscar wasn't satisfied. The Spaldings also had small owls that nested on tops of their porch posts and would sit on your shoulder.

Miss Ella Chelf had a dog that went to church every Sunday to wait for her to go home.

Oscar and Gene May had a crow that could talk. This crow stole coins from the Methodist Church collection plates.

Nicknames

Bradfordsville could be the capitol for nicknames. Here are some samples: Skunk. Babe, Bugger, Hot Shot, Bird, Duddle Bug, Duck, Jim Crack, Cuji, Dagwood, Buttermilk. Preacher, Shug, Spivey, Fuzzy, Bunt, Tater, Coot, Pee Wee, Cap, Big John, Tootsie, Cricket, Duffy, Dock, Pom, Bootie, Pappy Dick, Tackhammer, Pokey, Fluffy Chicken, and Toby.

Biggest Foot in Town

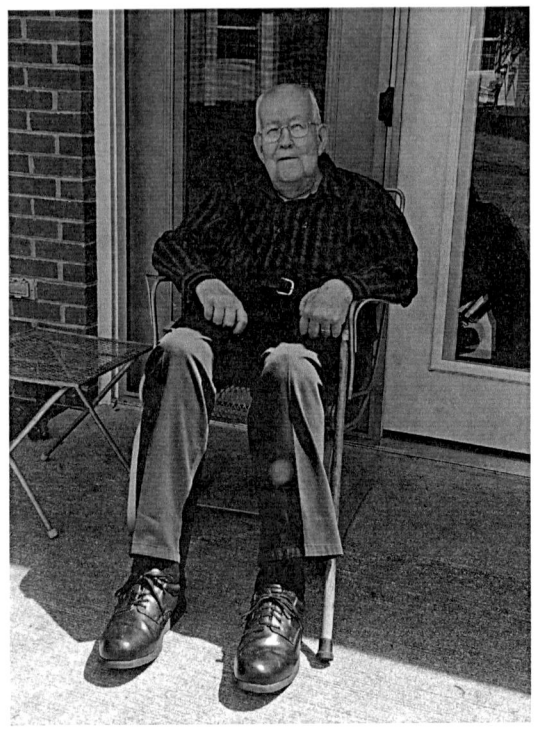

Ed Wilson wore a size 16 shoe which has now grown to size 18 in his '80's!

To Pick Up a Body

Rudale Cabell worked for the Don Drye Funeral Home for a time. One night he was called out into the country to pick up the body of a recently deceased person. It was dark when he arrived at the home. People were sitting around in the yard with only their dark shadows visible. Soft mumbles drifted in the night air as Rudale made his way into the house.

A lady was right inside the door and Rudale asked her where the body was located. She pointed to a bedroom and said, "In there."

Rudale entered the darkened room and cautiously made his way to the bed. He reached to lower the cover and a voice from the bed said, "I want a drink of wa-ter."

Rudale jumped a foot! That was enough to startle anyone!

Rudale left the room and told the woman that the person in the bed was still alive and wanted a drink of water. He said he was leaving as his services were obviously not needed. "Oh, no," begged the woman, "please stay a little longer because he'll be dead in no time."

A Little Early

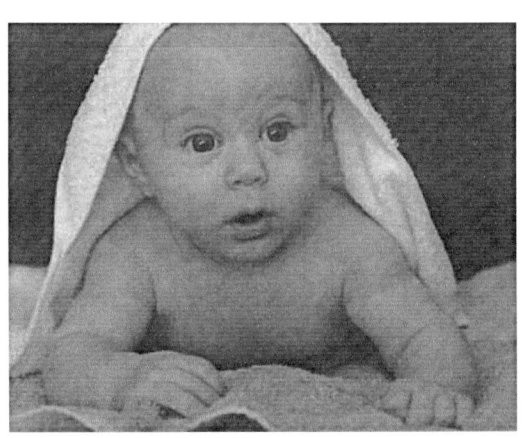

Moses Joseph Beard (1859-1953) was leaving his farm one day when he overtook his tenant walking down the road. He stopped to converse a little. The man seemed to be very upset and in no uncertain terms he said he was leaving and wouldn't be back. "What on earth has caused you to be so upset?" inquired Mr. Beard.

"As you know, Mr. Moses," answered the man, "I haven't been married very long and last night, my wife had a baby!"

"Ah, now," Mr. Beard said in a soothing voice, "The first ones are liable to come anytime, and after that, they tend to come more regular."

Knowing that Mr. Beard had several children, the tenant thought he surely knew what he was talking about, and so he changed his mind and went back home.

Tar Baby

Most of us remember the Uncle Remus story about Br'er Fox entrapping Br'er Rabbit with a doll made out of tar. Br'er Rabbit kicked the contraption and became stuck. That's when Br'er Rabbit begged not to be thrown into the briar patch.

We had a little boy, Milton, dressed as Tar Baby at one of our Halloween school festivals. He was the son of Bowen and Laura Belle Grubs. Of course his face and arms were blackened but his parents didn't stop there. They blacked his little bottom and tore out the seat of his pants to display their handiwork. Here was a little three year old kid running around in bib overalls, a straw hat and the seat of his pants missing with his little black behind exposed. It certainly had a shock effect even for Halloween. (I doubt a costume like that would be accepted today and some questioned it even then). That night the little boy earned the nickname "Tar Baby." It's a nickname Milton Grubs carries even today.

Make a House Scream

Rosin is used to wax the strings of guitars and fiddles, but Bradfordsville boys found it could be used to make a house scream. Jimmy Wooley says that Cap Hancock was the best at it that he had ever seen.

Cap would tie a string to a nail on a loose siding plank. He then would stretch out the string and run the rosin up and down it. That caused a screeching, screaming and vibrating sound that could be heard a mile away. Inside a house that suddenly starts screaming makes a person go mad.

Jimmy said you had to run and hide after doing this to keep from being shot!

Constable Ray Allstot

Roy Murphy came to town on most Saturdays but on this one he happened to cross paths with Constable Allstot. It began when Roy messed up in Billy Black's store. Some said that maybe his drinking caused him to stumble into some merchandise and scatter it about. The constable was called to get to the root of the problem. Roy wasn't going to wait for any interrogation, so he ran.

The constable saw him running across the field behind the rock-faced schoolhouse and called for him to halt. (Perry Morgeson watched from his family's porch). Roy had come to a wire fence and was climbing over it about the time Constable Allstot shot. The shot rang out and Roy fell.

Perry thought that Roy was wounded, if not dead. Suddenly, Roy got to his feet and kept running. Constable Allstot didn't "get his man" that day!

AIR HORNS

J. W. Russell had a new Hudson loaded with chrome, a very flashy car. To top it off, he installed two large air horns on each front fender.

Example of an air horn

He was known to sometimes have a little "too much under his belt," especially on Saturday afternoons. When this happened, he would drive his fancy car to the top of Fairview hill. He would head for downtown and would start blasting those huge air horns.

He wouldn't stop at the intersection at Drye's store. Running about 80 miles an hour, blasting those horns, he sped through Bradfordsville causing a lot of commotion among the people. Impressible young boys thought those antics were a royal show. Everyone else was glad he never killed anyone, including himself.

It was a Bradfordsvillian sight to see and horrendous sound to hear!

Halloween Pranks

Every Halloween the boys would try to think of ways to outdo themselves from what they had pulled off the former year. One particular Halloween, Jesse Purdy, Sam J. Murphy, and about twenty others topped all the Halloween pranks up until then, and perhaps forevermore.

They took a farm wagon apart and reassembled it on top of Skunk Mullin's grocery store. Then they went to a burned out building, and with all twenty or more of them, they pulled and dragged an I-beam and planted it across the door of Charlie Phillips' restaurant.

The next morning an early crowd, mostly those boys, was waiting to see how Skunk and Charlie would react. Skunk viewed the wagon on the roof top and calmly said, "Now boys I don't know how you did that but it's time you got it down and don't tear up my roof."

Charlie reacted differently. He chose a few foul words to address the problem. He offered a few threats and made some demands. None of that gave the boys inspiration enough to remove the beam. In fact, the beam stayed in place for two days. No one could go in or out of the restaurant because it had no back door.

Charlie got Sam Conder to hook a chain to the beam and try to drag it from the door. Sam's truck and the chain couldn't do the job. Finally, all twenty or more of the boys got together and cleared the beam from the doorway. In a few days, the boys were back in Charlie's restaurant playing the jukebox and the pinball machines. All was forgiven, but the event was too good to ever be forgotten.

Horse Sense

Many consider a dog to be a man's best friend, but Steve Garten would have to say that a horse was his best friend. Steve trained his old horse to go to town and do his shopping.

Steve lived across the North Rolling Fork River. Many times it was not convenient to stop work and go and get supplies, so what was a man to do? Steve was very good with that part—he trained his horse to cross the river, go to Bradfordsville to one of the old stores on Main Street and do his shopping.

Steve would put a note in a pouch on the side of the horse. The horse would take the note to old Mr. Black, who would read the note and take care of what was needed—be it nails, cheese, or whatever he was in need of. The merchant knew that Steve would take care of paying him when they saw each other.

Mr. Black would put the merchandise deep in the pouch, give the horse some feed and then slap the horse on the rear to get it started as it returned without a rider back down the streets of Bradfordsville to cross the river and get the needed items back to its owner, Steve Garten, who did not have to quit work to take care of short errands that had to be done.

Reason to Court Again

A certain man by the last name of Followell lived on the street above the Christian Church. He died and left his wife a small bit of cash. She bought a new Studebaker for her son.

That car was advertised as having an indestructible transmission. Her kid proved them wrong. He would get up to 50 mph and shove it into reverse. He did it enough times until he wore it out. Soon after, he totaled the car. She then bought him a new Kaiser. He totaled it. Funds were dropping, so she went down to a Ford. He tore it up, too.

The next thing we knew, she dyed her hair red and "set out" courting again. Everyone said it was because she was out of money. Her kid was just one of several speeders we had in town, but the only one who drove his mother to become a redhead and start courting.

Eight-Year-Old Flies

Wonderful events can happen at church revivals; sometimes feats are quietly carried out but are specular anyway. We point out such a feat that happened one night in 1963, during a revival, when 8-year-old Freddy Marlow jumped out a second floor window at the Bradfordsville United Methodist Church. (See picture.)

Freddy had gone upstairs to the boy's restroom and the door jammed with him inside. He yelled for help but the congregation was singing and didn't hear him. Feeling panicky he solved his problem as only an 8-year-old would do: he climbed onto the window sill, looked down at the ground two stories below, and jumped! Down, down he went, meeting the ground below with a hard thump but on his feet.

After regaining his breath, he felt some bodily aches. He reentered the church and had to explain to his mother what had taken him so long. At first, she thought he had jumped from the lower bathroom. (Why, he wouldn't have jumped from that window because that was the girl's bathroom!) She didn't believe him until he showed her the upstairs window from which he had bravely leaped. He was then taken to Mary Immaculate Hospital for a checkup. Miraculously, his body had only been jarred and nothing was broken.

Could he have been given invisible wings for his downward flight? He was young, innocent, and had chosen a church window, and many souls were nearby worshiping. Many believe he was given an unearthly gift for his flight that night. How else could he have accomplished it?

What's in My Bed?

When June Cabell was a teenager, she was spending the night at her Aunt Rhoda and Uncle Ernest Wooley's home. She found Aunt Rhoda's feather duster and put it in her uncle's side of the bed, down under the covers with the feathers turned toward the head of the bed. Then she hid behind the door.

Before long her Uncle Ernest climbed into bed and rammed his feet into those feathers. Instantly, he started yelling, "What's in my bed? What's in my bed?" throwing the covers in every direction and jumping sky high, landing on the floor.

To make matters worse, there was a lot of laughter coming from behind the door.

Forgetter and Wading Boots

Billy Black owned Bradfordsville's middle county store. (Gribbins' Store was farthest down. Black's store was in the middle. Owen Harmon's Store was closest to the Christian Church toward the upper end of town.) Mr. Clyde Wilson worked with Billy Black for many years.

Clyde said that Mr. Black would come in the front door and pick up the first box he saw. He had no idea what he picked up or why he picked it up or where he was going with it. He would set it down. And before he was out of the aisle Clyde would ask, "Billy, where did you go with that box of nails you had?" Mr. Black would ask, "What box of nails?" Clyde would say, "The one you picked up when you came in the front door." Mr. Black would reply, "I don't remember picking up any box or nails!"

Clyde in exasperation one day exclaimed, "Billy, you can't remember anything!" He replied, "Well, why have a forgetter if you can't use it?"

Perhaps there's a lesson in Mr. Black's response that many could use when needing to use our forgetter and forget the slight wrongs people have committed against us. (Just saying). Billy Black was a good man who was a Baptist and treasurer of the Bradfordsville Baptist Church. He was always concerned about the welfare of his neighbors.

Bradfordsville is low lying to the intersection of the North and South Fork Rivers as they join together to form the Rolling Fork. For this reason, the town has suffered many floods. It was during one of these floods that this dear Baptist, Billy Black, decided to check out the high waters in the lower end of town. He put on his high wading boots to do so.

He was making good progress as he waded along in the two-foot water. In front of Miss Lyde Wright's house he stepped into a deep ditch and, shockingly, found himself in water up to his neck! He was in deep water and deep water was in his big boots! If not for his head, it could have been said that he was immersed for the second time!

Sweet Susan Mann

Susan Mann was as sweet a woman as ever walked on this earth. She of all people didn't deserve to be on the receiving end of a prank. But kids will be kids and sometimes deserving has nothing to do with it.

Ernest and Rhoda Wooley's grandchildren spent many weekends at their house. One Saturday, the youngsters, who were around 10 years old, (Rhonda and John being 9, Jim, Jr. being 10, and Gary at 8), found a pair of plastic legs. They dressed the legs in stockings and high heels, and then they found a brown wig that could add zing to the effects of their creation.

They went down to the main road and threw it in a ditch, leaving most of the legs with shoes sticking out in plain view. They then threw in the wig. They hid and cars passed but no one stopped. When the children tired of watching for a victim, they began playing another game. That's when they heard sweet Mrs. Mann come to a stop.

"Are you hurt?" Mrs. Mann inquired, leaning out her car window. No answer.

Speaking louder Mrs. Mann anxiously asked again, "Are you hurt?"

At this point the children decided it was time to confess their crime to this kind lady. "It's a dummy," they yelled. **"It's a dummy!"**

John Penn   Rhonda Penn   Gary Wooley   Jim Wooley, Jr.

At that, Mrs. Mann's vision became more accurate, and the sweet lady pressed down on the gas pedal so hard the wheels spun before getting grip and surging the car forward. As she drove away, it might be surmised that her thoughts were not as sweet as when she first stopped.

A Car! Where?

There were some shenanigans that happened in Bradfordsville that seem too hard to believe. In fact, this story requires some witnesses before we even considered printing it. Turns out that not only one witness, but two, have come forward to declare they saw it with their own eyes Those witnesses are Suzanne Cundiff Stelbach and Bob Wilson. It involves a car belonging to Suzanne's uncle, David Drye.

David was a student at Transylvania College and owned a yellow Jeepster. Halloween night some pranksters managed to position that Jeepster on top of the electric and telephone lines. No one can recall how it got there or how it was removed. But once seeing a car on top of power lines is a memory never forgotten.

On another Halloween, all of Mrs. Edna Drye's porch furniture was placed on those same electric and telephone wires. Bob remembers them as being a swing and rocking chairs.

It could only happen in Bradfordsville.

Night of the World's Demise

It was Sunday night, Oct. 30, 1938. Pauline Crowe had turned her radio to CBS at about 8:12 pm and heard that a Martian invasion was well underway in New Jersey. If anyone had ever observed Pauline Crowe at a Royal Aces ballgame, one would know that she could become extremely excitable. To hear that aliens had landed and were gradually making their way across America put Pauline into a hysterical panic.

The Methodist Church was holding services when Pauline rushed into the church, approached the preacher, interrupted his sermon. She whispered the terrible news in his ear. He immediately closed his sermon and announced to the congregation that Pauline had heard on the radio that the world was coming to an end. Naturally the people became very excited. Sixteen-year-old Louise Gribbins was in the audience and it was from her that we heard this story.

The Gribbins family went home but Louise and her fifteen-year-old brother, Buddy, decided to ride in a horse pulled wagon back to town. That was where most of the excitement seemed to be and they wanted to be a part of that. Besides, Louise had lost a glove in the fervor and she wanted to find it.

There was great excitement going on when they arrived. Stories were getting wilder and wilder. People were afraid that perhaps their souls were not prepared. There were those trying to calm the crowd by telling them it was a fictional radio show that Orson Wells was broadcasting. It took a long time to convince the scared citizens but finally the truth was accepted. A great relief settled over the community and life continued.

"Back at You" and Run!

Phyllis Hollon and Vickie Drye were close friends. Sometimes their actions could veer toward impulsive. So it was one day when they went strolling in bare feet through the school yard and ended up at the bottom of the front rock wall that bordered the street. Everyone knows that it isn't wise to agitate a bunch of drunks. That is, if any previous thoughts are given to it.

As they walked along the wall, they heard a car stop directly above them. They backed up against the wall to hear what the occupants might be saying. They soon realized they were listening to a carload of drunks. Then, a bunch of beer cans were thrown over the wall directly where they were standing.

Much like a game of Annie Over, the girls picked up the cans and hurled them back. The throwers did not graciously receive their cans and began cursing, saying "Who threw those cans? Where did they come from? Who's under there? We'll get you #%*@!"

The barefoot girls wasted no time running toward the Hollon's apartment above the bank building. They took a short cut through the abandoned lot behind Dr. Drye's office. They ran like the English at the Battle of New Orleans. They ran through the "briars and they ran through the bushes where the rabbits couldn't go," and they ran over the rotten planks and rusty nails. They made it home.

After thinking about the incident, they couldn't help but laugh about what those drunks might have thought when those cans came flying back up into the air. Could the drunks have thought the cans hit a trampoline that bounced them up again, or maybe a town ghost that made its home under the wall and  didn't tolerate cans in its front yard. Turning all that over in their minds threw the girls into fits of laughter.

Tossing Compliments

Old Man Will Hasty was sitting on his porch back by the river. He saw five good looking ladies coming up the road from the Raney's house. He looked at them and said, "There come five mighty fine looking girls up the street." One of the girls replied, "We're sorry that we can't return the compliment to you." Not to be outdone by their response, he said, "Oh you could, you could, if you told a damn lie like I just did!"

Put It on my Tombstone

Jess Abell always said that when he died they would put on his tombstone, "There lies the truth" because it never came out of him when he was living.

Don't Keep Goldia Waiting

by Evelyn Wooley Mardis

In the late 1950's, Evelyn's mother, Goldie Wooley, had an appointment to get her hair done at Geneva VanDyke's Beauty Shop. Her husband, Charles, dropped her off. After she had her hair done, Charles was not there. She waited and waited for him, and eventually she got agitated. She called Pickerill Motor Company in Lebanon, talked to Sonny or Jake, and asked them to bring her a car. She wanted a new car, but not a blue car, being she didn't like blue.

A short time later a new tan Dodge was delivered. When Charles got home, the car was in the driveway. Charles was upset. He couldn't believe Goldie had done such a thing. He was so upset that he went to see his daughter, Evelyn, told her all about it and decided to spend the night instead of going home. He was more upset that Goldie had written a check on the wrong bank to pay for the car.

The matter was corrected and a few weeks later, Charles was so pleased that it was though he had chosen the car himself. Weeks later, he called Evelyn and said, "Let's go on a trip to Knoxville and drive the new car," which they did.

Pretty Vase for the New Table
told by Fern Cox

In the 50's several ladies in the community belonged to the Homemaker's Club. Every month they met in a member's home where they shared recipes, watched demonstrations by the county extension agent, caught up on better health issues, and made some lovely craft pieces for their homes. Some of the members were Frances Tucker, Madge Cox, Lillian Purdy, Evelyn Purdy, Susan Mann, Rhoda Wooley, Carrie Mae Wooley, and several others who were truly interested in homemaking. It was during this period of time when most farmers' wives did not work outside the home and running the household was their fulltime occupation. Also, it was during that period of time that women were conscious of always appearing ladylike. They appeared as proper as could be when visiting, shopping, or just going about.

Every month the club would take a little trip to a nearby town to see whatever attractions the town might have to offer. They ate lunch together and enjoyed shopping.

The group knew that Madge Cox had just purchased a new dining room suite that included a beautiful table. On one of their trips they all went into an antique store. They were browsing about, examining the many lovely items on display. Susan spied an unusual vase. Picking it up, she remarked to Madge, "This vase would look so pretty with flowers in it and sitting on your new dining room table." Madge gave it a glance but turned her attention to something else.

Susan thought the vase was the perfect fit for the new table, and she kept talking about it and the other ladies just weren't responding to anything she said about the vase. Even the proprietor stepped away and didn't try to sell the "vase" to Susan who was showing so much interest in it. Finally the group left the shop.

As they were walking away, Susan said to Madge, "Didn't you think that vase would have been pretty on your new table?"

Madge answered, "Susan, that "vase" was a man's urinal chamber."

Growing Up in Bradfordsville

recollections by Ed Wilson

Boy Scouts

Bob, my brother, and I loved climbing the knobs around us. Our house faced White Knob (so called because it was covered with ¼ inch to ½ inch slivers of slate). It appeared white from our house because little vegetation was growing through it.

Ed Wilson & Bob Wilson

We were "Boy Scouts" for about a year. Our troop never did much other than meet regularly, say the pledge to the flag and repeat the Boy Scout Pledge.

I remember taking a hike

to White Knob. We climbed that knob until we found a spot to set our tents. Then we built a fire and cooked supper. I don't remember what we ate, but it was good.

Then we sat around the fire and told ghost stories until bed time. We went to bed and slept fairly well and woke up at the crack of dawn.

Not one of us, including the Scout Master, had a watch. It could have been nearing "noon" for all we knew. We got up and cooked a great breakfast. Then we closed "camp" and hiked back home.

I remember walking in our house just as our Mother and Father were ready to eat breakfast. We sat down and ate as though we hadn't eaten in weeks. It was 6:00 am!

The Scooter

At some point in our early lives we decided we wanted to build a motorized car. Our Dad found a half-horse power, gasoline powered Briggs & Stratton "washing machine" motor and bought it for us for $25.00. It was during the 2nd World War and anything made of metal was difficult to find. My Dad talked with Wes Richardson, owner of the DeSoto/Plymouth Dealer there in town. He finally persuaded us that a motor scooter would be more practical and easier to make. SO, a motor scooter was in the works.

We ran that thing all over the country. It would go on level ground and it would go downhill, but it would not go up a hill no matter how slight the grade. We would get off and run along beside it until we were at the top of the grade, then get on and ride again.

Later, we decided to request that people planning to give us Christmas presents give us money to buy a new 1-½ horse power B/S motor. It was advertised to develop 2.1 horsepower at full throttle. Again, it was during the war and it cost $90.00. I'm sure it would be the equivalent to a five horse power engine today. It was heavy cast iron. I remember being down at the Desoto/Plymouth garage when the new motor was put on that scooter. Bob was the first to try it. He went up the South Fork, turned around and came back into town with the thing a full throttle. He ignored the stop sign and turned right to go up a hill we had never before been able to climb. It went up that hill as if it was level ground. I discovered it would even go up that hill with me on it. We had 12 inch solid rubber wheels. All over, it lacked stability. The handlebars were from a wrecked bicycle. It had a ½ inch galvanized pipe going down to the "fork" holding the front wheel. I remember riding it on a street parallel to ours. The front wheel hit a slight dip. It jerked the handlebars out of my hands, causing them to flip forward into the road in front of me. A welding job was needed again.

Jeanette Wooley & Bob Wilson on the scooter

I'm not sure how we learned of it, but Bob heard that someone had a Cushman Scooter in his barn with a broken flywheel. We bought it and repaired the flywheel. It had two gears, an automatic clutch, big balloon tires, and was truly ready for the road. It would go 45 mph. The scooter itself was made for two people. We used to use a rope and pull two bicycles behind us and go to what we called the "Second Iron Bridge" to go swimming.

In the summer of 1952, Bob and I got on that scooter and struck out for Indianapolis, Indiana. It was a 200 mile trip each way. Somewhere in Indiana, the chain on the scooter broke. We did not have a spare link. Bob remarked "I read in a Popular

Mechanics Magazine of a man riding a motorcycle in Alaska when his chain broke. He had nothing with which to fix it and decided to cut a wire out of a fence to get the chain together again. SO, Bob cut a small piece of wire from the fence. I don't know that it lasted a half mile when it broke again. There was a road construction crew there and Bob showed them the wire he had used and asked if they had a stronger wire. They did have such a wire, and we were able to get to our destination with no further trouble. We stayed with our oldest sister and her husband (Lois and Leland Anderson). We went there each summer and painted a white picket fence around their trailer home to earn our keep.

We started home on Sunday after church. Somewhere along the way we needed gas. There were hardly any gas stations open on Sunday. We finally talked a man into selling us a tank full of gas. I'm guessing it was less than 50 cents. After a while it started getting dark. The scooter had a headlight, but it soon went out. We could see by moonlight but I'm certain other cars had trouble seeing us. THEN, miracle of miracles, here came our Mother and Father toward us. We were waving our arms and shouting to enable other cars to see and hear us. (It was summer and the windows of cars would have been down.) To the end of their lives, I think they thought we recognized them in the dark. At any rate, they stopped. I got in with them and Bob went in front to have the lights of the car to show him the way. Also, it would go a tad-bit faster with only one person on it.

The next summer, following my graduation from high school, I went to Indianapolis to work. While there, Bob came to visit, again riding the scooter. The next morning as I left for work, Bob rode up to Chicago and on up to Milwaukee before returning home on that scooter.

The Water Tank

My Dad took care of the town waterworks. We lived in the upper part of Bradfordsville, but there were several houses above us. At the very upper end was a knob. On that knob was a 50,000 gallon underground water tank. Every few days my Dad would have to go up there to check the amount of water in the tank and to add chlorine to make sure it was safe to drink. The only way we had of knowing when the pump needed to be started was when the water pressure at our house got weak… which probably meant the customers farthest up the hill were out of water.

My Dad wasn't always available to start the pump himself, so Bob or myself would take the car down to the river bank, unlock the pump house and start or stop the pump as needed. (The water came from a spring on the far side of the North Fork River.) Neither of us was near driving age, but we knew what needed to be done and did it.

Speaking of that underground concrete water tank, it had a ½ inch thick iron lid and I think was about 4 feet square. Even in the winter it was warm under that lid and those purple stinging scorpions were always under that lid. My Dad used a 20 inch leaf spring from an old automobile to stick under the lid to pry it up. The pad lock was then put under the lid to prop it up so we could get our fingers under the lid to lift it up.

Of course, we always used caution and looked under the lid to be sure there were no stinging scorpions where our fingers might be.

Swinging on the Grapevine

I remember going up that same knob (with the town's underground water tank) with Bob, Parley Bright and a few others. Walking near the top someone saw a grapevine hanging down. I don't remember if I was the only one who didn't swing on that thing, but I feared disaster if I tried it. Bob, and at least some of the others with us, would grab that vine and run like crazy to the edge of the bluff and jump off into nothingness, swinging out over nothing until they came back to land several feet away. Then they would do the same thing to get back to where they started. It looked like fun, but it wasn't for me.

Shoe cans

It didn't take a whole lot to entertain us. We used to take a "Pet Milk Can" (Evaporated Milk) that still had both ends of the can attached. (We also used some larger cans where a punch had been used to drain the contents of the can.) 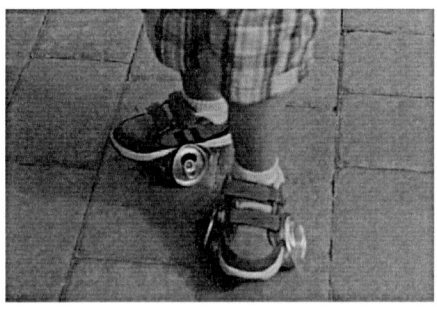 We would stomp our heels into one of two cans and then do the same with the other foot. Then we would clomp around enjoying the noise of our new "shoe savers."

Sparkplug

I remember being in the barbershop at home. J.C. Guthrie (a distant relative) told a story that had us all cracking up. He told about two little boys trying to start a gasoline powered mower. They were having no success.

JC said, "If you want it to start, you have to hold the sparkplug."

One of the kids said, "NO, that would shock me."

JC said, "Then hold it with these pliers."

He said the kid took them and took hold of that sparkplug while the other kid pulled the rope starter.said, "So help me, a spark was jumping from that kid's big toe into a tin bucket sitting on the ground by his foot."

Some Bradfordsvillians in these Stories

Back Row: James Tucker, Sam J. Murphy, George Purdy, Spivey Harmon, Fuzzy Whitehouse

Front Row: Pete Purdom, Maurice Cox, Bobby Wilcher, Kenneth Ewing, Jimmy Wooley, and B.H. Crowe

LEGENDS & GHOST STORIES

The telling of scary tales has been popular for thousands of years. Today we rely more on movies and television to have our spines chilled. Still, scary stories remain interesting to read or hear, and so we will entertain you with a few within these pages.

The nature of ghost stories is that they are to be repeated, told by one generation to the next, to be passed from parents to children, and from them to their children.

So if you've heard any of these before do not feel slighted.

It simply means now it is your turn to pass them on.

My Encounter with an Angel

As told by Allen Anderson

When I was in the army I was a tank commander in the 4th Cavalry. This one afternoon our troop pulled into an area where we were to spend the night. When a tank outfit did a sit-up for the night, all the tanks would be arranged in a circle with each facing out. The command vehicles, maintenance and mess vehicle were always inside the circle. On each tank there were four people: loader (who loads the gun); driver, (who drives the tank); a gunner (who fires the tank gun); and me, the tank commander. One person had to be awake and constantly watching what goes on in front of the tank. Every hour the command vehicle would radio each tank for a situation report. If nothing was going on in front of your tank, you simply said, "Sit-rep, no change."

That day we had been rolling since day light and everyone was worn out, so when we did our "sit-up" I decided I'd let the crew sleep and I would stand watch that night. Usually we took two hour shifts, but that night I let them sleep. When I woke everyone the next morning I noticed I was sick and had a fever. I was burning up. I sent my loader to get our Lt. and he came over in his Jeep. He took one look at me and told his driver to take me to the Aide Station. When we got there the medic said, "Get him to the field hospital."

The next thing I knew, I was on this bed covered with plastic, and I'm nude laying there being sponged with alcohol by two nurses and a doctor. I was freezing, shaking all over the bed. They had two huge stand-up fans blowing air on me. They told me that they almost lost me. My fever got to 105 degrees and they had to cool me down.

After that, they put me in a bed in a ward where there were about 15 other sick people. It was night and everyone was asleep but me. I would drink one glass of water and throw up three (or so it seemed). Sometime in the early morning an old heavy-set woman, who looked the way my grandmother used to look, came in with a mop and bucket. I was having the dry heaves at that time. She came straight to me and asked if I had stomach trouble. She spoke to me in Germen and I answered in English, but we understood each other. She said if I wouldn't tell anyone there, that she would give me something to make me well. I promised that I wouldn't tell anyone. She said, "Not a doctor or nurse?" I told her that I wouldn't tell.

She went out the door and came right back in. She had a cup and a saucer with some kinda thick black stuff in it. She said for me to drink it all. I did. Then she took the cup and saucer, mop and bucket, and left. I fell asleep immediately.

Next morning, some soldiers came in with a cart with trays of food for our breakfast. I felt so good that I got up and helped hand out the trays. The nurse came in and seeing me out of bed, she hollered for me to get back in bed because I was sick. She said, "We almost lost you last night, you Kentucky Hick!" I asked her about the cleaning lady. She said there were no cleaning ladies. The doctor told me that a crew of soldiers cleaned up for them. They dismissed me from the hospital that morning not understanding how I got well. That cleaning lady was my angel!

David Edelen,

Mayor of Bradfordsville 2018

Light in the Narrows

Retold by David Edelen

The narrows, the road or path that leads from Gravel Switch highway nearly a mile over to the Liberty highway near the Old Lick Slab, is a very secluded area, even though it is very close to town.

One night back around 1915, Harry Edelen, George Edelen, and Chap Noe were bringing horses over from the slab of Old Lick to Gravel Switch Road. The road was nothing but a path, and all the thick and hovering trees made it appear even more ominous. The pre-adolescent boys began their trek though the dark hills to get the horses back to the barn on the North Rolling Fork.

Flashlights had not been invented or at least not used in this area. Suddenly a weird foreboding round light appeared right in front of the boys. The small white beam appeared as a small bright flashlight would appear today. They knew they must get home, but they were not at all happy about following that strange light, but if they did not, they were more apprehensive about facing their dad and uncle and being late. So they decided to follow the light. It led them over the hill and down through the creek, seemingly knowing which turns and valleys to go in as it led the boys to their home.

After what seemed like an eternity of fear, the boys got a glimpse of the dark of their barn, but the brightness outside shown through the cracks between the wood slats of the barn, so the boys were able to hang the bridles and put the horses in their stalls.

By this time the boys were so unnerved that it was all they could do to put the horses up and make their way to the house. They knew the wrath of their uncle and dad would be severe if the horses were not put way properly. So they did what they were taught and then started toward the house. The light had gone in front of them all through the knobs and had even lingered at the barn, but it did not go toward the house.

The light proceeded to go toward the North Rolling Fork River, across the river, over the bottoms, and then over the knobs, never to be seen again.

Light at the Chimney

Maggie Edelen had just delivered her son, Carl, and the doctor said that Maggie was not going to make it. Many in the area came to stay with Maggie during her last hours of life. (Her father had not come. He had made the remark that he had heard so many times that she was going to die, and she hadn't done it yet). The house had several people inside, and many more outside as darkness filled the hollow.

Oscar Spalding was one of the persons standing outside. (Now Oscar was one of the most respected and trustworthy men in Bradfordsville). He was standing near the chimney where inside Maggie's bed was near. Oscar said that he glimpsed a light at the base of the chimney. Suddenly he saw the light go swiftly up the side of the chimney and flew right up into the sky.

Oscar went to the door, and those inside said that Maggie had just died. "I knew that she had left," he said. "I knew it from what I saw at the chimney."

Grave Digger

Nette Perkins told of a woman she once knew. This poor lady's young son died and she was grieved beyond consolation. Every night the woman would go to the cemetery and dig up the body of her son and kneel, and pray over it. She prayed that God would resurrect her child.

Each morning, the family would have to rebury the boy. Finally, the family locked her in the house to keep her from repeating this sad ritual. From time to time, she would escape and she continued digging up her precious son and praying over him. There seemed to be no stopping her and finally the family sent her to a lunatic asylum.

Mamie Thurman

There is a Bradfordsvillian ghost that can be heard wailing on Murder Mountain near Logan, West Virginia. She is Mamie Thurman, the wife of Alvin "Jack" Thurman. (Jack was the son of William Harvey and Annie Thurman). In 1924, she and Jack had moved to Logan from Bradfordsville, Kentucky. Eventually, Jack became a policeman there and Mamie worked at different jobs, two of which was a secretary at a car dealership and as a teller at one of the banks.

Over time it seems that Mamie became more of a party girl than a serious working girl. A local newspaper described her as "the well-known Logan club-woman". She was popular and well-known among the wealthy of the community, due to her beauty, outgoing personality, and loose conduct. Though married, she was apparently having an ongoing intimate relationship with Harry Robertson, a city leader.

F. Keith Davis, in his book, <u>The Secret Life and Brutal Death of Mamie Thurman</u>, describes it this way. "In the summer of '32, Mamie Thurman was executed in gangland style on a miserably rainy evening. Her soft complexion was viscously marred and disfigured from being battered and suffering powder-burns from gunshot wounds. Her throat was slit, leaving a thick ugly slash from ear to ear. Her slender, shapely body was dumped like rubbish at an illegal dumpsite."

Blame for the crime was finally laid on an African American citizen, Clarence Stephenson, a handyman. He was sentenced to life in prison without the benefit of parole. Many to this day believe that Stephenson was framed.

Mamie's death certificate filed at the courthouse states that she is buried at Logan Memorial Park in McConnell. Harris Funeral Home that was in charge of the body has records that show the body was transported to Bradfordsville, Kentucky. It is also said that during the night, a prominent business man from Logan paid $1,000 to have her body moved to a Chauncey cemetery. None of these cemeteries hold the body of Mamie Thurman.

Even today, there are those who claim to have seen Mamie along the roadway in a blood-soaked polka-dot dress, always veiled in mist, and drifting in and out from sight. Others say they hear her bloodcurdling screams coming from the mountain on which she was murdered. Mamie's spirit seems to be restless and searching for something she has missed. Meanwhile, her husband, Alvin "Jack" Thurman is lying at peace beneath the soil in Old Liberty Cemetery, alone and without Mamie beside him.

Phantom Horses

told by David Edelen

Willie Mullins lived way up Traverse Creek Road; he lived way, way up the road, past the end of the creek all the way to the top of the hill, the top of the knob, the top of Chestnut Flat Knob. This knob runs into Casey County by Little South, by the edge of the Big South Fork, from Rocky Ford, to the back of Penn's Store, from Jonah Creek to White Oak, to the town knob of Bradfordsville. Oh, yes, he lived way up there. The knob where Willie lived was referred to by many as a "straggler knob," where you can get lost and not find your way out for days if you are not familiar with the lay of the land.

Willie built a little house on the top of the knob, where peace and tranquility of the ages could be found. It was a remote area where a spring bubbled water from the rocks with cool refreshment on a hot day. This spring was one of those strange things that God had provided, with no explanation of why a spring might come forth at the top of a hill instead of the bottom, and why it never ran dry even on the hottest and driest of dry days.

Traverse Creek was one of those weird areas where tales of hidden gold being buried in the hills, and a valley where Cherokee Indians camped in as they were led on the trail of Tears to their Oklahoma destination many years earlier. This is the area that Willie chose to build his cabin in the late 1800s.

All was peace and quiet until one day Willie heard it. It was at first a muffled far away sound that kept getting louder and nearer. Finally, Willie could identify the sound of one horse which then became two, then three, and then a whole herd all running, racing, ever faster and nearer. They were coming right for his cabin, around the curve of the trail, till it seemed they were about to come right in front of Willie. Willie was frozen to the spot where he stood. Then, just as surprising as was the approach, was the sound of their retreat, slowly getting quieter and more distant as they faded and faded, till there was no sound at all.

Family and visitors heard the horses. Even Willie's grandson, Buster Morgeson, heard the sounds. Was it the horses of the Indians as they tried to hide their treasures during their ill treatment on the "Trail of Tears"? Was it the scuffling and ruckus of the ship builders as they prepared lumber for ships at the mouth of Traverse Creek during the 1800s?

No one knows, they only know that they heard the beating hoofs many times and could never explain the mystery, only that it sounded like horses running past the house on their way to somewhere beyond Willie Mullin's cabin.

The "Japs" Have Landed

During World War II, while the war was going on, there was little media coverage available for folks to know what was happening.

Mrs. Josie Dever and Mrs. Eulalia Sweazy were walking to visit a neighbor. Mary Lane was in her home busy with her household duties. She was sweeping and dusting and had picked up a small rug to shake it outside when she looked through the open door and saw a man standing with a hard hat on and some kind of machine in his hand that appeared to be a machine gun. Her heart leapt into her throat. She looked across the fields and there were other men with hard hats in every direction. She figured it out. The 'Japs" had landed! She had to warn her neighbors.

As she went running she could see what appeared to be swarms of men moving about with those hard hats and many were carrying those "machine guns." She ran as fast as she could until she finally overtook Mrs. Dever and Mrs. Sweazy. She was grasping for breath but was able to hoarsely speak, "The Japs have landed! The Japs have landed!"

Mrs. Dever and Mrs. Sweazy could not make sense of what Mary was trying to tell them, but decided whatever it was, they should find out. Going back from where Mary had come, they spotted surveyors everywhere, surveying the road from Gravel Switch to Bradfordsville.

One summer night Brother Tony Conley took some teenagers for a marshmallow roast down on the river bar at the First Iron Bridge. What follows is a ghost story that was told that night.

COLD AS CLAY

There was a wealthy farmer in this area who had a beautiful daughter named Julia. His wife had died when this child was born and perhaps that was the reason he loved his daughter so very much and wanted nothing but the very best for her.

The farmer had hired a handsome man, Perry Smith, to care for his large herd of fine horses. Julia and Perry fell in love. The farmer felt that Perry was not a suitable mate for his daughter, and so he sent her to live with his sister in Casey County. He hoped that in time Julia would forget about Perry Smith. A few weeks after Julia was sent away, Perry Smith took ill and died. Some say that he died of heartbreak. The farmer chose not to tell Julia about Perry's death, hoping that by the time she heard she would have forgotten all about him.

Time did not erase the love that Julia had for Perry, and each day she dreamed about him and longed to see him again. Her longing seemed to come true when she saw a fast approaching rider coming up the lane toward the house. It was Perry Smith riding on one of her father's fine stallions. He told her that she must hurry, that her father had sent for her.

Julia quickly gathered some things and in a matter of minutes she was behind Perry, holding tightly to his waist with her cheek against his strong back. They had ridden a few miles when Perry said that he had a terrible headache. Julia felt of Perry face and remarked, "You are surely sick because you are cold as clay." She took a lacy handkerchief from her pocket and tied it around his head.

In a few hours they arrived at her father's house, and Julia slipped hastily down and ran to the door. Her father had seen her running up the walkway and he flung open the door to greet her. "I came as quickly as I could when I heard that you wanted me!" she exclaimed.

"I'm so glad you are here but I didn't send for you," answered her father.

She said, "But Perry told me that you wanted me to come!" Looking around they saw that Perry and the horse had disappeared. They thought perhaps he was putting the horse in its stall. When they reached the barn, they saw the stallion in its stall and it was wet with sweat. Perry was not there.

The father went to the home of Perry's parents, hoping they could explain everything to him. The parents were as baffled as he. They said their son was buried in the family cemetery on the hill behind their house. They decided to have the body dug up. So with neighbors helping, the grave was reopened. The coffin lid was forced open. Inside was the reclining body of Perry Smith and around his head was Julia's lacy handkerchief.

Mama's Visions

by Jeanette Wooley Wilson

Was it a sixth sense or something more sinister? Whatever it was, Mama had it. It wasn't mean, whatever it was. It was just mysterious and amusing. Daddy called her "Mammy Yokum" whenever her "feeling" came. (There used to be a comic strip called Lil' Abner, where his mother would go spinning in a trance and was able to foretell the future). Mamma didn't spin but from time to time she would tell us of an event that was coming our way.

So often, without any prior notice, she would announce that her brother, T. C., was on his way from Illinois to visit us, and sure enough, in a few hours he would drive up and she would already have something special baked for him. But there was one time she made a different kind of prediction, and that one was kind of scary.

She always got up before Daddy. He would crawl out of bed when he heard the oven door slam. (Mamma was noisy in the kitchen). This particular morning in 1950, she announced when he came into the kitchen, "Miss Ella Chelf died last night."

"Where did you hear that?" Daddy asked.

"I didn't hear it like you normally hear things," she said. "I had a feeling that came over me last night that she had died."

We had a saying in our home when we couldn't understand where the other was 'coming from,' and that was, "You're crazy." That's what Daddy told her.

"Wait and see," she warned and went about finishing up breakfast.

It was a cold day and after milking, Daddy was sitting around the house, just being lazy for a while. Early afternoon my Uncle Charlie came in the door. (Uncle Charlie was always in a hurry, and he was always pushing my daddy and Uncle Henry to move a little faster).

"Ernest, we've got a grave that will have to be dug cause there's been a death in Bradfordsville last night," Uncle Charlie announced.

"I know," Daddy answered, "Ella Chelf has died."

"How'd you know that?"

"Rhodie told me."

"Rhodie told you! How did she get the word so quick?"

"She had one of her visions last night and she had a strong feeling that Ella Chelf died."

Uncle Charlie shook his head and said, "That beats all."

"I know," Daddy answered.

Grave in Old Liberty Cemetery

Gold on Travis Creek

Told by Ed Wilson

Clyde O. Wilson was born in 1893, on Travis Creek, 5 miles from Bradfordsville, up the South Fork (Hwy. 49) towards Liberty. The house where he was born was approximately one-quarter mile from Highway 49 on Travis Creek. He told this story many times.

When he was a small boy, an Indian woman from Oklahoma came to that section of Kentucky with a map and this was her story. When the White men chased the Indians from that part of Kentucky, her ancestors had buried some gold, fearing they would be captured and have it stolen from them...at the same time hoping they would eventually be able to return for it. The map showed two tiny creeks coming together, forming a slightly larger creek. In that area where they joined, there was a knob. Up on that knob was where the gold was buried. They had carved the face of an Indian on a birch tree. If you sighted down the nose of that Indian...where it touched the ground was where the gold was buried.

Local residents introduced her to a well-known hunter from that area, believing that if anyone could help her find the location, he could. The two of them walked those hills for several days and finally gave up. She returned to Oklahoma.

Sometime later, someone observed that the James Wilson house was located in that "V" where two small creeks came together, with a knob behind their house. THEN someone spotted a large birch tree with a crude carving on it. Clyde always said it was more of a triangle in shape…but, sighting down the nose, he would go stand where the gold should be.

Naturally we kids asked, "Did you dig to see if gold was there?"

His response was, "No; no one ever believed her story!"

Even as kids we were thinking, "Why would anyone come all the way from Oklahoma with a map and such a story if there was no truth to it?"

He said, "I've plowed the top of that hill many times and I never hit any gold!" He would have been plowing with a horse or mule, and it is highly unlikely he would have gone deeper than six inches. If gold was buried there, it surely would have been deeper than that!

When my younger brother (Bob) and I were nearing high school age (probably in the late '40's), we decided to go up there and dig. We had one bicycle. We both got on it with a pick and a shovel and rode 5 miles to Travis Creek. We climbed that hill behind my Grandmother's house (My Grandfather died before I was born.) There was nothing but roots covering the top of that knob. There was absolutely no way we could dig through them.

So, we gave up and went back home and as far as we know, no one has ever found that gold!

The Spirit of Bradfordsville

It flows in your blood. It is buried memories that surge periodically, bringing smiles or lingers with a bit of sadness. It is what we were, what we are, and what we will remain. Being a Bradfordsvillian is all of that. Once the spirit of this town grips your heart, it never lets go.

We've traveled back to the time Bradfordsville was first settled, to the time of the long hunters and Indians and forts and cabin homes. We've remembered the hardships of the Civil War, and as we read, we envisioned the townspeople rebuilding their beloved town. We went through the boom years of the early twentieth century, and then the Depression, and the fires, and the loss of our school. We've remembered our childhood games and pranks and antics that we and our friends pulled. We've recalled some of the stories our elders told. Now we pause. We are now in this moment of time.

Bradfordsville is somewhat like an old woman who once was vibrant and now seems she needs more rest. Her main street is quieter. Her school doesn't contain those former students studying to better their tomorrows. Her doctor's office is empty. Her post office has shorter hours. One of her church buildings is an Art Center and another has been torn down. Persons driving through might perceive that she is pulling the draperies and ready to lie down. How wrong they would be.

Her school building has been restored to its former grandeur. Inside the walls are reunions, receptions, meals, singing, auctions, cake walks, music, pageants, and much more. Up on the hill, a new Christian Church has been built and it is active in delivering the message of Christianity. Down at the lower end of town, the Baptist Church is constructing a new building in which to worship and serve God. Bradfordsvillians are proud of its popular restaurant, The County Store, which has people coming from far and near to enjoy its fine cooking. There's a Learning Center and a Community Building, a fire department, town water works, sidewalks, and an active mayor and city board. There's the Super Save with groceries, snacks, and tables where citizens can just hang out and visit. There are other businesses that serve the community in various ways.

Not so many grand houses have survived and some grocery stores do not now exist. But the spirit of the people is much alive. The citizens strive to better their community and make life fuller for each other. Until that spirit dies the town will live and serve. Until that spirit dies, there are many of us who so gladly proclaim, "I'm a Bradfordsvillian and I'm proud of it!"

Jeanette Wooley Wilson

BRADFORDSVILLE SHENANIGANS POINTS OF INTEREST

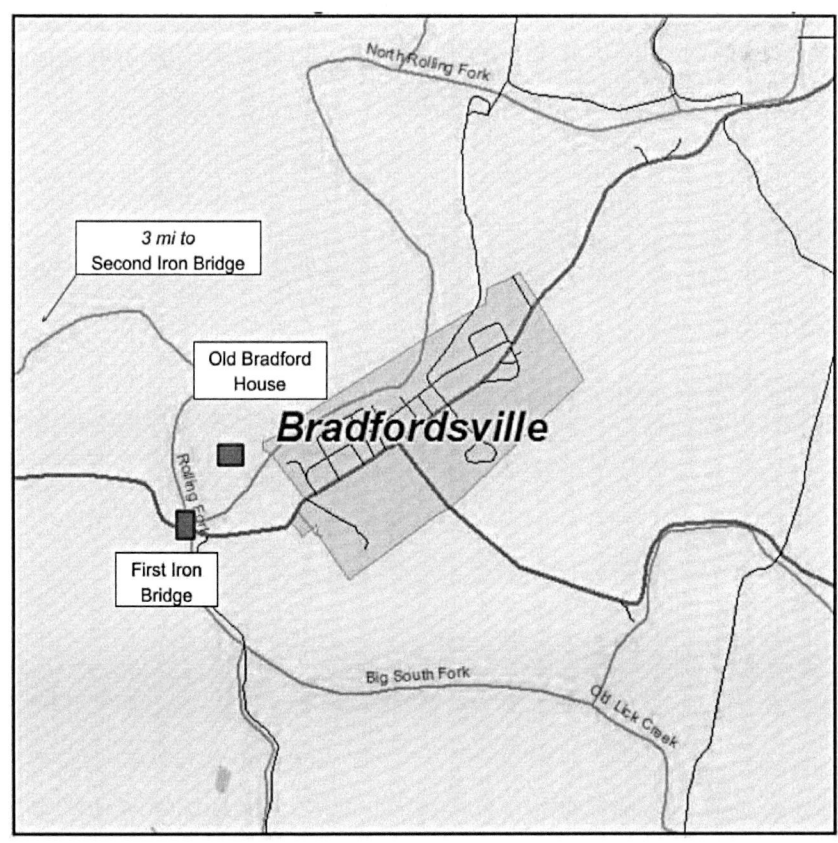

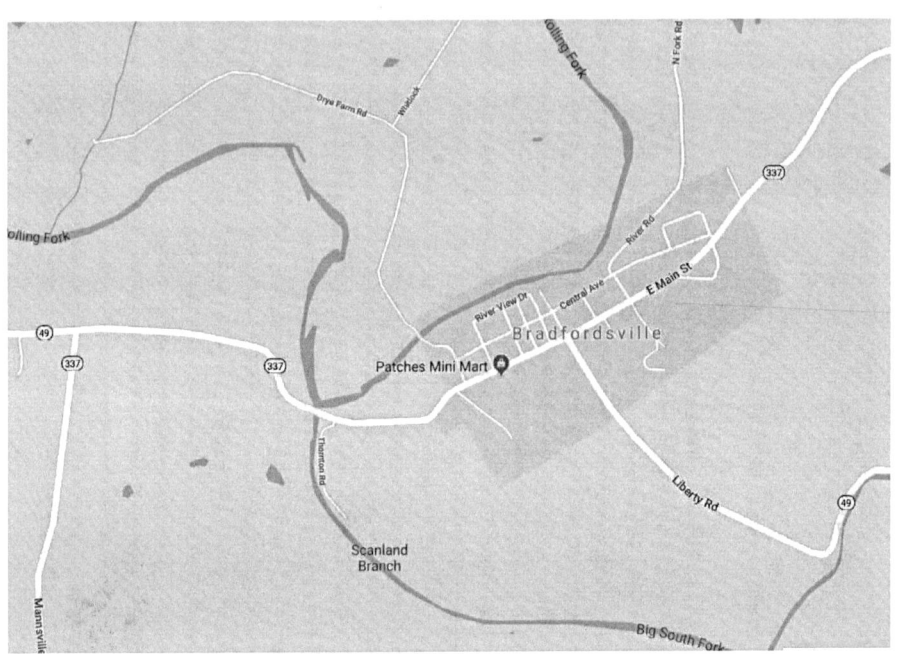